Horse *as* Teacher

The Path to Authenticity

Lisa Dee
Wendy Golding
Karen Head
Holli Lyons
Stormy May
Mary Beth Meyers
Melisa Pearce
Kathy Pike
Anna Twinney
Susan Williams

Marilyn Schwader, Editor

CLARITY OF VISION PUBLISHING • PORTLAND, OREGON

For more information, visit www.HorseAsTeacher.com

BOOK DESIGN AND PRODUCTION BY MARILYN SCHWADER
COVER PHOTO BY TONY STROMBERG
EDITOR: MARILYN SCHWADER

ISBN: 978-0-9824494-0-0
Library of Congress Control Number: 2009926146

Table of Contents

Foreword

The stories in this book are a perfect illustration of today's spirit of the times. Yes, on one level they are simple stories of love, trust, and honesty, which will make you smile, laugh, and cry in turns. At the same time, they tell of the transformations that are now taking place on a personal and global level. Each person within these pages that took the leap of faith with horses to a brighter future is a trailblazer and role model for us all. Their evolution is our evolution. Their story is our story.

The remarkable and talented writers who contributed the stories embody too, the spirit of this new milennium. The idea of a group of successful and respected teachers and clinicians from the same field coming together to collaborate on a project such as this would have been unthinkable 10 years ago. They have become a human herd, where the group mission is as important as any individual's message. The power of community is demonstrated in this collection of authors.

What we learn from the pages of this book is that the wisdom of the horse should be recognized. As you read the different stories, listen carefully to the "horse sense" and insights contained therein. While the stories come from amazing women that have been brave enough to open their hearts, the wisdom has come from the amazing horse teachers in their lives.

The ability of a horse to act as a mirror in their interactions with humans is the basis for equine-based learning. The horse's instinctual need to detect incongruities in strangers forces an individual to be honest about their feelings. This in turn requires that the person connect with the truth that lies within. This is our natural state. A state of peace where we are able to live true to ourselves without contradiction.

In these uncertain and confused times, it is clear that as a species we humans are not walking our talk or living our truth. The world is crying out for guidance and help and, indeed, we need to move to higher levels of consciousness if we are to avoid making the same mistakes over again. The path to greater personal and global happiness lies in listening to one's heart and paying closer attention to the relationships in our lives.

Horses and humans have traveled together since the dawn of time. Horses have pulled our carts and our ploughs and carried us into battle. We now live in a different era and they are no longer our "work horse." This century will surely see freedom for the horse. We live in more enlightened times and it is obvious that control of the horse by means of force and pressure is just not necessary. Horses may be the most forgiving of creatures, but just because we can impose our will upon them, does it mean we need to or should?

If these stories illustrate anything, it is that we need to re-evaluate our relationship with the horse. It was the trust that these writers and their clients placed in the horses that led to the breakthroughs that changed their lives. We are learning that if we as a species are to move to the next level, we need to place our trust in the horse and become horse conscious. When we accept the horse as our partner and learn to listen, we will open ourselves up fully to all the wisdom and higher levels of connection they offer.

Recently, I remarked to Kathy Pike, the co-founder of *Horse as Teacher* and a contributing author, that it is the responsibility of those of us who seek a better world for the horse, to speak up when we see injustice, as the horse cannot speak. She laughed and replied, "Mark, every time a story, article, or book is published on this subject, the horses are talking *through* us and to us, loud and clear."

Enjoy the stories, listen to the horses, and be the change in the world.

Mark Mottershead
Founder – HorseConscious
The new paradigm in horse human relationships
www.horseconscious.com

Preface

When I was seven, my parents finally succumbed to the continual requests from my brother, Tony, and me to have a horse. We lived on a South Dakota beef farm and Tony had a dream of becoming a cowboy – and I just wanted to ride. Penny was a copper-colored Shetland-cross pony. She was beautiful. My hair matched her coat, making it easy to pretend my parents had found her just for me. I had visions of us galloping for miles, like horses in the movies, carrying me wherever I wished to go.

Penny was stout and small, and well into her twenties by the time she came to us. Despite her age, she was energetic, willful, and irascible. Looking back now, I see that she was perhaps mirroring the young whippersnapper that I was. She was also probably not at all happy to be babysitting two very rambunctious children. She and I always seemed to be at odds. After a number of instances where Penny bucked us off or tried running under low-hanging branches to get us off her back, my dad finally put her out to pasture. She seemed relieved to be there.

Sam, a buckskin quarter horse was our next horse. He was calm and friendly, in sharp contrast to Penny. Tony trained him for working cattle, but most of my time with Sam was spent exploring the wide-open pastures surrounding our farm. I imagined myself as a cowgirl in the Wild West, pretending I was on a trail ride, exploring new lands. I loved galloping across the flat fields, the wind blowing through my long hair, riding bareback, and hanging onto his dark mane as he carried me on wings of dreams.

When I was twelve I was diagnosed with scoliosis and was fitted with a brace to straighten my curved spine, greatly diminishing my ability to ride. At the age of 20, I had a stainless steel rod attached to the length of my spine, and my riding days came to an end. It was a great loss. I felt that if I couldn't ride these elegant animals, I couldn't bear to be around them. At the time, there didn't seem to be any other reason to maintain the connection. And so I stopped spending time with horses.

As the years passed I channeled my energy into creative endeavors, with a focus on writing. I eventually became a writing coach and started publishing the *Guide to Getting It* book series, a collection of 10 synergistic collaboration books similar to the *Horse As Teacher* book series, written by life and business coaches.

About the same time the book series was getting started, I experieenced a sequence of serendipitous events, leading me to study with a shaman, a breath worker, and a divination practitioner. Each teacher continued to lead me on a similar path of understanding and working with intuition, energy, healing, and consciousness. The horses continually came to me in dreams and shamanic journeys, but I never quite understood why.

One day, twenty-plus years after I had left horses behind, I received a call from my friend and coaching colleague, Kathy Pike. She was giving her first workshop in Equine Facilitated Learning and invited me to attend.

The workshop was held at a ranch near Prescott, Arizona. There were enough stories from that weekend to fill a book. I experienced the horses teaching – and healing – on levels I had never experienced in all of the many modalities of personal growth, healing, and human awareness that I have studied. The intuitive, energetic connection these sentient animals were capable of was phenomenal. I had never understood the mystical nature of horses. Until then, I had no idea of their gentle power and ability to teach humans about being their true self. My thoughts went back to Penny and what she was probably trying to tell me about who I was trying to be with her.

I was mesmerized by what I learned in my sessions in the round pen with those beautiful teachers. Just as important, I was with the horses again. Until I was standing with them in the workshop, I hadn't realized how much I had missed their presence in my life. Their smells, their energy, their beauty came rushing back to me in a wave of familiarity.

What I learned that weekend dovetailed magically with my studies of shamanism, breathing, and energy work. Everything seemed to be melding effortlessly with the teaching from the horses.

I returned home, excited to combine all the disciplines I had been studying and start working with the horses as healers. But although my heart said yes, I was still allowing the false voices in my head to lead the way. Instead of finding ways I could start working with the horses, I seemed to find all the excuses for why I couldn't. The horses continued to speak to me, never completely leaving my thoughts, but my focus was elsewhere and so the pull to work with them remained a dream.

Four years later, I received another call from Kathy. This time she asked if I would be interested in publishing a collaboration book series highlighting horses as teachers to expand human awareness. The memories from our workshop came flooding back, and this time my heart took the lead; I was finally in a place to explore this work more deeply.

It has been my privilege to collaborate with the talented and dedicated authors who wrote their stories here. They have reminded me of the healing gifts and gentle mirroring a horse provides when you are willing to let the lessons in and open up to following your heart.

The stories in this collection will move you to tears, make you laugh, remind you of your first brush with love (in the form of a horse), and most important, connect you with your soul; because that's what horses can do when you are willing to embrace what they so naturally and beautifully reveal to you.

The authors come from a variety of horse backgrounds, but there is a common thread – they all see the simple truth that these magnificent animals, through their presence and grace, can raise our consciousness, peel back the layers to uncover our true selves, and show us how to shine with brilliance.

I thank Kathy Pike for introducing me to the emerging field of learning and healing with horses, for suggesting this book series, and for her tireless efforts to educate people about the ability of the horses to guide and heal humans. I thank the authors for baring their souls in the stories they tell. I thank the horses for being, which in the end, is the most simple and profound lesson they teach.

Marilyn Schwader, Editor
Founder of Clarity of Vision Publishing
www.clarityofvision.com

Heart Whispers

By Kathy Pike

Singapore

His back was warm and the color of caramel. His pony height made it easy for me to place my hands on top of him. The heat from this body softly crept into the palms of my hands.

Singapore was his name. The program manager at the non-profit said he would not be working with the disabled children that day because his back was out and he was in pain.

After being away from horses for many years, I was eager to spend time with any one of them. Although I had never worked on a horse before, I instantly offered to do some massage with Singapore. The owner was agreeable. I walked down the quiet aisle of the barn. All of the other horses were eating the last of their breakfast. When I entered the stall, Singapore did not move. He had finished the bulk of his meal and did not seem interested in picking over the small remains.

His head hung low and his eyelids were heavy. I took a few steady breaths to center and reach a state of intuitive awareness, just as I had done hundreds of times with my human massage clients. All awareness of our surroundings faded into the recesses of my thinking mind. The soft October sun crept into our space. My eyes soaked in the gold, cream, bronze, and wheat colors that sparkled as the sunlight rose, moving across Singapore's body. I became present only to this horse. He was already present.

My sense was he needed a gentle touch, so I let go of my earlier, eager, ego-based desire to "fix" him. Instead, I chose to offer comfort, my presence connecting as deeply as possible with his. I raised my hands from my sides, and with palms face down, moved one to his spine just below his mane at his withers and the other above his lower spine. I felt the connection and flow of energy between us. My heart became full and the physical boundaries between us began to fade away.

I whispered to Singapore, "You don't need to hang onto this. Let it go." Instantly a single loud hard crack intruded on the stillness of the paddock; bone snapping against bone, the joints in his spine popped and released. My body felt a slight jolt as a wave of hot energy moved through my body.

Singapore exhaled a long slow breath, his head hung low as he began to lick and chew, seemingly content, not one foot moving, free of resistance. My eyebrows raised in amazement. How easy and swiftly he had released his tension compared to the time it would take a human, during a massage session, to do the same. It took no physical effort on my part. My undivided attention, spacious mind, and heart-felt intention for his well-being had provided him the space to release his tension. He responded.

This moment between us sunk deeply into my consciousness. How different life would be for humans if we could be more like Singapore and reach this place of complete trust, if we learned to release the resistance to what is emotionally or physically creating disharmony and live fully in the present moment. Why do humans hang on so tightly when letting go can happen in an instant? Oh... to be more like a horse.

I walked away knowing I had received a gift, but not really understanding completely what the gift was – yet. But I trusted that time would tell.

Kairos

Years later my life had evolved from my human-based healing in massage and energy work, into a thriving life coaching practice that included horses as partners or co-facilitators for human awareness.

It was February and cooler than I thought it would be in the mountains south of Tucson, Arizona. I was facilitating a four-day equine-based learning program. Each day we focused on exploring the different chakra within the human body, while engaging with horses. The group was warmed by a low sun that filtered through the tree branches tipped with tight spring buds. The grass was brown without a hint of spring, though it didn't seem to matter. We were all happy to be in the desert with the horses.

That day our focus was exploring and igniting the fourth chakra – the heart, the energy center that represents how one experiences giving and receiving, the quality of the breath, and their sense of inner balance. The heart chakra bridges the energy of the physical world into the spiritual world and offers a place for both to work as one.

One of the workshop participants, Joanne, selected to work with a solid black Percheron. These horses have served mankind for centuries with their strength and surefootedness, carrying men to battle and plowing fields.

This Percheron was named Kairos. He was by far the largest horse I had ever seen. Well over 17 hands high and weighing over two tons, his solid, massive body evoked a deep essence of his genetic history. The weight of his physical body alone provided a calm grounding for the group. His gentle nature made time stand still. His slow-moving, solid black muscular mass called us to him. Kairos, in Greek mythology, signifies a period in between, a moment of undetermined time in which something special happens. By simply being near Kairos, several people reported a deep sense of communion and connection to something that was beyond words. Kairos' complete focus and slow, gentle gestures moved people to the depths of their consciousness.

During Joanne's round pen session I coached her through a deeper level of self-awareness in her body, mind, and spirit. We stood outside the round pen while Kairos stood patiently inside waiting with his gaze intently on her. As my client slowed down her mind and became more aware of her inner landscape, her feelings, sensations, and energy, the other participants seated nearby stopped fidgeting and also became more present. I felt Kairos' presence already protectively wrapped around us. Each moment felt as if we all were dropping deeper into our awareness.

When I asked my client what she might like to experience with Kairos, she replied that she wanted to deepen her connection with her heart. He stood waiting, unmoving, not even blinking an eye.

She entered into the round pen while Kairos held his ground in the center. Softly and slowly she walked around him and stopped slightly in front of his right side. I stayed on the outside of the round pen, but was slightly to the front of his left side.

The activity around us, the normal ranch noises, suddenly became non-existent. I could no longer hear the birds in the trees; they too had become silent. Stillness filled the air and a blanket of timelessness softly fell on us. Then it happened. I could feel his focus on her, the energy of his presence and intention penetrating deep within her heart, the space between them turning into diffused waves of invisible warmth. As my gaze went to her, to my surprise, I felt the invisible stream move from her heart and into mine. I could not distinguish if it was intentional, as her eyes were still on him. I absorbed the expansive state of my heart; it felt as if it had grown three times in size.

The wave of pure life force energy washed through my whole body as I felt a burst of energy behind my eyes and tears form. The tears were not of sadness, grief, or fear, nor were they tears of longing or vulnerability.

Instead, the tears were the expression of a life force itself, as if I were being connected to something beyond myself that was actually part of myself. They were tears of recognizing my own spiritual source and the interconnected energy of all beings. My eyes gazed to Kairos and settled softly onto his body.

In that moment an unspoken word passed from Kairos to my client, to me, and then back to Kairos. The unspoken word felt like a complete book of knowledge, a sense of expansion and depth much greater than anything I have ever experienced with any other horse. Time stood still. There were no questions to be asked and no answers to be explored. That empty moment simultaneously contained all the expansive wisdom of the universe.

My client stood still, and so did Kairos, the other participants, and me; we all bathed in the stillness. Several minutes later she walked to him, offered her palms together in a Namasté prayer of gratitude, and then walked lightly back to the gate. Kairos, never moving a muscle, remained the pillar of strength, a grounding rod, a channel to the world beyond.

People who commune with nature may have experienced these delicious moments that are beyond words and physical worldly existence; the moments when all is one, and the wisdom of the ages sinks into one's cells. A few moments of this level of connection creates a powerful restoration of the soul. I seek these moments that are bottomless, wide in girth, and endless in time; where all of me becomes part of all that is.

Joanne shared with us that she felt her heart in a way that she had never felt before. Large and alive for the first time, she felt the possibility and immensity of pure love, love without thought. All of the participants in the group reported a similar experience. Kairos, with his sensual, prehistoric, and calming energy, had given us all a ride into the infinite state of connection.

Many equine-based learning programs focus on "doing" something with a horse in order to have an equine experience. Once at a demonstration, a participant criticized my philosophy and approach. She claimed the sessions were not "experiential" enough. The woman declared that for a participant to truly learn something, he or she needed to touch or physically interact with the horse. There is great value in learning through the doing, touching, and moving; and often I find even more value in practicing "not doing." The horses' most natural state of being is a peaceful state. They enjoy being in their herd, resting in the sun, and grazing. They are masters of the art of doing very little.

Kairos had transported all of us beyond our normal reality by inviting us into a state of non-doing, or "being." Without physical movement of his body, he had carried our consciousness into another realm of understanding. In that moment, each individual reconnected to a part of her self and the world beyond in a powerful spiritual experience.

Physical touch and movement does not always quantify a true experience. Powerful moments that invite us to pause, such as the one with Kairos, are often what help us become aware of our hearts and the feeling of authenticity that rises from this place. An experience is defined by recognizing and gaining knowledge or comprehension through observation or interaction. Achieving an experience can happen by simply "being" versus "doing."

I believe we can achieve deep levels of self by simply "being." It is our doing nature that puts us into our heads, fills us with agendas, and removes us from feeling from the heart. When we choose to "be," we choose to breathe, feel, observe, and accept the moment as it is, and as we connect with another. There is no time for judgment or analysis. Authenticity comes from the heart, not the busy mind that is rationalizing, manipulating, positioning, planning, thinking, worrying, and justifying.

Corazon de la Montana

Singapore and Kairos had generously taught me to connect to the depths of my authenticity through connecting to my heart and being present, by giving and receiving heart-based energy. Not all equine experiences are of this nature. In reality, horses have the capacity to stretch us in many ways emotionally, physically, and spiritually.

A little black horse taught me to experience and fully comprehend the opposite of authenticity – the experience of a racing mind, unchecked emotions, and an ego attached to agenda, a time of losing connection to one's heart.

The horse, all of 14.2 hands high, is close to a "pony" status. The program directors at the prison's Mustang training program said the 5.5 year old recently gelded wild horse was halter-broke. I don't really like that word, "broke," nor was I even clear what halter-broke training really included. But I believed him anyway.

When the Mustang arrived, I anticipated it would be an emotional moment. Finally I was doing something for the wild horses. The little black horse shuffled off the trailer, his back hooves hitting the hard pavement with a thud while his front hooves dragged against the hard metal floor of the trailer, finally hitting the ground. He took two authoritative steps away from the trailer, his head held high and proud as he slowly turned 180 degrees to get a good look around him, scoping out the situation, unbothered by his new environment. The transport man simply said, "Here's your horse," and handed me the lead line.

Then my insides began to shake as I realized that the months of talking about adopting a wild horse was now a reality. His black head, just slightly higher than mine, stayed high and proud as he took in his surroundings. I felt invisible next to him. He felt big, dramatic, and strong. All thirty of the ranch horses walked to the edge of their paddocks to watch his arrival. Ears forward, they were curious: Who was the new boy on the block?

I felt rushed as eight workshop participants were waiting for me to return to a program I was leading. The closest and best place to put the big little black horse was in the round pen. In we walked and the transport man closed the heavy metal gate behind us. I draped the rope over my arm as my hands steadily moved toward his head to release the halter. I noticed how worn both the lead line and halter were. A fleeting thought moved through my mind, "Did it really matter if I return this ratty halter?" My mind was racing with all sorts of thoughts, questioning everything.

I had barely touched him, barely taken the time to get his attention on me. I had little to no time to walk him around a bit so he could stretch his legs and realize I was his new person. As my fingers began to undo the halter's buckle, a fleeting thought moved through my mind, "Should I be doing this?" My logical thinking brain said, "Yes." He is, after all, halter broke. Out of the halter he slipped and a realization ran through my mind, "I shouldn't have done that. Man, I am in over my head."

I named him Corazon de la Montana, "heart of the mountain" in Spanish. He was brought in from Montana, the genetics of his herd having been traced back to the Spanish conquistadors, some of the few herds left with this lineage.

I began the approach to our relationship gently. He received his meals each day from me. I would hang out with him while he ate. When he was done I would walk around him and scoop up the manure. Some days I simply hung out on the outer side of the round pen. He would reach through the pen and smell me, placing his nose on my head, or the flesh at the base of my spine where there was a gap between my jeans and shirt. These small gestures filled my heart; he was making friends with me.

However, he was not so keen on me getting close to him. I could move to him and stand quietly by his side, just an arm's distance away. If I lifted my hand to stroke his withers, off he would go in a rush, in fear that I was going to leap onto him and kill him. In his mind I was still a narrow-focused predator.

For the next month I tried everything I could think of and all the techniques others offered or I read about to get next to my new friend. Lucky for him he was in the round pen so he always had somewhere he could go to get away. He certainly didn't seem "broke." He was a little horse with a big wild spirit fighting to keep his last few days of freedom, even if it was only sixty feet round.

At times I felt I should give this horse up to a more experienced trainer, for I felt I had little to offer. I would not recommend the adoption of an older wild horse to any inexperienced individual. It is unfair to both.

I used the natural horsemanship methods I did know to work his feet and body and to control and influence his movement. At times he would turn into me, offering me his face, snorting and throwing his head. He seemed bigger than life itself as his agitation and frustration radiated from his being. Sometimes he would lower his head and show softness. When I would become more assertive, he would also become more assertive. His little body did not lack presence, and truthfully, he intimidated me and he knew it. He had my number. I was not skilled enough to earn his trust in the round pen. In fact, I often felt I was creating more distance between us. We continued to navigate each other and our relationship until the ranch owner began to pressure me to get him out of the round pen.

Corazon was my teacher. I had spent hours teaching my clients how to be present with the horses, when riding or working with them on the ground. We worked with aligning one's emotional state with a clear sense of purpose and intention, but always remaining connected to the energy of the heart. Personally, I had developed a higher degree of presence with many different horses, even working through my fears of riding after being dragged by a horse in my twenties. However, this little horse with his wild, proud nature was rattling my core. In trying to connect with him, I experienced joy when he would reach out, and anger, humiliation, shame, fear, and frustration when he would not give me the response I wanted. An emotional roller coaster overrode any of my previously gained skills on being "present."

I wish that I could say that one day the bridge was gapped and he came to me, of his own free will, and offered his friendship in some gentle, mysterious way. It did not happen. He took every chance he could to fight for his last moments of freedom. Every day, his gaze was on the horses in the far pasture, the ones that were grazing at liberty and in a herd.

Everyone gave me advice; some of it was helpful, some of it not. In any case, things were not moving fast enough.

The moment I am most ashamed of happened near the end of my attempts to halter him. Our relationship had grown with baby-steps. He had enough trust in me to allow me to scratch his withers, back, and up his neck. He was beginning to understand that I was not going to hurt him. We could stand together when my hand was lower than his eyes and giving him enjoyment. At these times my body would relax; I felt comfortable. Yet, I knew I had to get that halter around his head. I could feel everyone at the ranch waiting and watching. The round pen became a pressure cooker. My ego feared the failure.

Finally one day, I got very close to haltering him. I had bought a new halter, a light green color that would look lovely against his strong black head. As I lifted the halter around his head I felt relief – finally it was going to happen. My ego would be satisfied. Then I noticed a shiny piece of metal at the end of the strap that would go through the buckle. Pretty, but not helpful. Just as I was about to slip the strap through the buckle, I felt a wave of anticipation move through me. Then the flashy metal tip of the strap hit metal buckle and sent a slight chinking sound into the air. Corazon threw his head, gave a slight rear, and bolted. In all of my frustration and anger I threw the halter after him, and "gave him a reason to leave." Big mistake.

My emotions had taken over. I had blown it. I had given him a reason to go, which only made it harder for him to return. I felt the lowest I had felt in years as my dark side, my anger and impatience, was exposed. There was no one to blame or shame except myself. I had become what I despised.

Shortly after the round pen incident, I hired a seasoned wild horse trainer to come to the ranch to help. I chose her because I knew she would focus on working with him with respect, not over powering him or dominating him, but helping him to see a solution.

She arrived on a warm and sunny, mid-summer Saturday. We started at 9:00 a.m. She too worked with him as I had. He never tired of the round pen movement; he had lived in the wild for five years of his life. He was fit and strong and could go forever. He would only let the trainer so close to him, just as he had with me. As soon as he saw the halter coming, he would take off. I sat outside of the round pen wrapped in worry and feeling that adopting this little black horse with a big wild spirit had been one big mistake.

Eventually we moved extra panels into the round pen and shrunk the size of the round pen itself. I could see over time that Corazon was thinking about what we were doing. His eye never left her, even when he would race away. Eventually the round pen space had been narrowed into a space of about four feet diameter. It was 3:00 in the afternoon when he accepted the halter.

At all times, Corazon offered me a true authentic response to life through his internal reference point. He was a wild horse trying to survive in the human world. I began to understand that he did not want to hurt me, but he wanted to know he was safe. His safety was dependent on my inner strength. I had to learn how to resource this place in myself, to become the leader he needed and to keep him safe in the human world.

For every two steps forward we gained in our relationship there would be one step back. Slowly we made progress. I continually had to examine how I asserted myself. The position or intent that I had allowed my inner frustration to move to – "I will give you a reason to run away" – did not work. What did work was asking him for cooperation with a neutral state of energy in my being, and holding positive possibility in my heart. For this to happen I had to work on myself. Some days I skipped away from our sessions together with joy, other days I left feeling completely hopeless, the worse days I left feeling a complete failure with my anger and frustration running me. Corazon taught me every day that I had to be stronger, more understanding, willing to fail, and I had to learn skills in order to work with him.

Corazon de la Montana took me on a path of seeing the dominating side of human nature – mine and others. When these moments would emerge, he would turn his gaze onto me, his dark, strong eyes unblinkingly penetrating my being. Then a thought traveled from him to me: "Are you sure you want this?" I got this same message when trainers, farriers, and other individuals that entered into our relationship did not seek to understand him first. However, because I felt I lacked the skills needed to handle him, I continued to let these individuals do so, therefore participating in what I now consider "lesser" ways of training and interacting with horses.

Eventually I came to the other side of my own darkness and found a stronger resolve in my own truth. I started to speak up for my horse and tell other very experienced individuals what his needs were and the boundaries of how he was to be treated.

Then, I almost lost him.

It was July 5th and the veterinarian kept insisting I put Corazon down. A block in his small intestines refused to move and my little wild horse was struggling with colic.

A rollercoaster of inner-turmoil racked my being and once again I felt helpless in relation to the expert and his recommendations. I had never been through colic with a horse before. The vet claimed there was nothing left he could do; the horse should be put down. Memories of Singapore came flooding through me. I gave Corazon the only thing I knew I could offer. I rolled up my sleeves and began to massage him, for hours. That night he passed manure. The next day I massaged him more; my friends arrived to help as my arms fell to my sides in exhaustion. More manure passed. The vet continued to insist that he would not live because the compaction was in his small intestines. Corazon's eyes drilled every cell of my being and I heard him again, "Are you sure?"

In the end, I found my inner strength, stood up to the vet, and with the help of a friend, took him back to the ranch. If the wild little horse named Corazon de la Montana were to die, he would die a noble death with his feet on the earth, the mountain air streaming through his mane, and surrounded by his herd.

Two seasons have cycled and nine months later Corazon walks to the gate to greet me and we nuzzle and say hello. When I see him I count my blessings and love streams from my heart to his. I now am part of his herd. He knows I can be trusted to do the right thing. My blessings also extend out to the fifteen people who supported the process of saving his life. This human herd taught me about generosity and support.

Horses are true to what they feel and experience, and respond accordingly. Horses teach me to be aware of my energy, intention, presence, touch, and heart. These qualities invite connection and harmony, create healing and expansion, and ignite cooperation in the toughest of times. This little black horse with a huge wild heart taught me that when I *trust* what I believe to be real from the depths of my inner being, that our path continues to grow and our connection deepens.

Regardless if an experience with a horse is soft and gentle, or rebellious and difficult, each time there is opportunity to practice mindfulness and awareness. It is a daily practice.

I cannot imagine a life without my horses. They bring peace on wooded trails, in grassy mountain meadows, and snowy pastures. Dancing with them brings me joy and my heart fills each time I see how they help my clients heal and grow.

Horses *are* my path. I choose no other. They are my teachers, and each day they are in my presence they help me to find my heart connection – my *true* self.

Thank you to the horses who have graced me with their presence and made these stories possible. Singapore was part of the Medicine Horse Program in Boulder, Colorado. Kairos lives at the Apache Ranch in Arizona, home of Epona Equestrian Services. Corazon de la Montana came to me through Ginger Kathrens, film maker, author, and founder of The Cloud Foundation. She has filmed the Pryor Mountain horses and a stallion named Cloud for many years.

About
Kathy Pike

During her twenties, Kathy spent most of her time mountain climbing, skiing, or biking the western states and Europe. While watching the glaciers calving on a river trip in Alaska, she realized it was time for her to return to civilization and serve others. Shortly thereafter she enrolled in massage school in California.

The next ten years of Kathy's life focused on developing her skills as an energy healer, intuitive, and life coach. In her late thirties, all of her experiences came together as she wrote her first book, *Pathways to a Radiant Self: A Journey of Growth and Discovery with the Chakras*. Coaches began to request to be trained in her methodologies and her next piece of writing, the *Mind Body Method Coach Training Manual*, emerged. Her coaching clients soon discovered the power of the processes Kathy had developed. Their truth, passion, and purpose emerged and her clients became empowered to make substantial changes in their lives.

Horses came into Kathy's life unexpectedly. After being thrown and dragged in her twenties, she had no intention of being around horses again. While writing her first book, a horse named Hope picked her and pulled her back into the "herd." Hope showed Kathy the possibilities of merging her coaching practice with the guidance of horses. Healing her own trauma through engaging with horses, she learned powerful ways to fully integrate mind, body, and spirit.

Over the past nineteen years, Kathy has worked with thousands of individuals and business teams to create positive change in their lives and relationships. Her second book, *Hope . . . From The Heart of Horses: How Horses Teach Us About Presence, Strength, and Awareness*, offers stories that demonstrate her depth of knowledge and passion about horses being viewed as sentient beings that have a special wisdom to offer humans.

She is proud to be the co-founder and a contributing author for the *Horse as Teacher* book series that supports talented teachers and clinicians, and raises consciousness around horses.

Kathy seamlessly blends her abilities to be practical with her natural intuitive and healing skills in working with her clients. Her background includes: graduate and trainer for CoachU, teacher at the Boulder College of Massage Therapy, and teacher for the Naropa School of Extended Studies. Her corporate programs included clients such as Microsoft, Dalby Wealth Group, Storagetek, and the Women's Vision Foundation, to name a few. Kathy has spoken about the power of the mind body connection and working with horses at several International Coach Federation international conferences, along with several regional and local organizations. Her articles have been published in over ten local and national publications. She is an Approved Instructor through Epona Equestrian Services.

Kathy now travels nationally and internationally to teach and speak. She resides in Carbondale, Colorado with her two horses, Moon and Corazon de la Montana.

For more information, visit www.coachingwithhorses.com or email moon@coachingwithhorses.com.

Crossing the Silly Bridge

By Lisa Dee

I remember the first time I heard my horse speak. The irony was that I heard her speak at a time when I could not hear much of anything. You see, the more pain I felt, the more I tried to block it out by creating noise. Until finally one morning, when I could no longer stand the deafening noise and the pain, the dam broke. What I had been so afraid of, happened. I started crying and I couldn't stop.

It was what I knew would happen and why I had steeled myself against it in the first place. But the flood of emotions that had built up over the years was finally too powerful for the wall I had built up, brick by brick, to keep the emotions at bay. The wall cracked. And big chunks of it fell apart, letting the flood of emotions pour over it.

I do not know how much time had passed. When I came to, the tears had stopped, leaving dry, crusted trails on my cheeks and my eyes had swollen shut. It was a good thing. I was not ready to see where I had landed.

In the dark, and in the quiet, I realized the noise had subsided.

I heard a voice: "Go to the horses."

In my exhaustion I was unable to move or react.

I heard it again: "Go to the horses."

I had wanted to run away many times, but I never knew where to run. Now I did.

When our hearts speak, and we listen, we find ourselves. It's just that simple. I did as my heart asked. I went to find the horses. Here, then, is my story…

Once upon a time I woke up… and found myself living the song, *All My Exes Live In Texas*. I did, after all, live in Texas. And had… several exes.

It was time to move. And change my life. And find a new theme song.

But where? The company had an office in New York City. This would be a logical move. It was hopefully the last logical thing I would do in my life.

There, surrounded by concrete, I was compelled to do something, ummmm... nature driven. Of course.

Walks through Central Park were not cutting it. What would satisfy my hunger?

I had it. It was time to live out every girl's fantasy. It was time to ride.

After all, why not learn to ride in the middle of Manhattan instead of doing this during my 12 years in Texas?

Fantasy is not logical.

I went to the famous stable that serviced Central Park. I was put on a very cranky horse and told to ride around in minuscule circles in an arena with five other very cranky horses all charging around in their own miniscule circles while dodging concrete pillars.

This was *not* what I had in mind. I continued my search.

I found an outdoor arena. It was big and had real dirt... and a view of the Empire State Building. This looked promising... in an urban sort of way.

I went inside and saw a picture of a cowboy-looking dude... something about Natural Horsemanship. Hmmmm, that sounded good.

So I signed up.

I really didn't understand what the guy was talking about during the lesson, but the horse was really great and relaxed as opposed to the other very cranky horses in the indoor arena being whaled upon by little girls with crops.

My instructor came to me as I was looking gooey-eyed at his steed and said, "You know, if you like this stuff, you should really go to the top to learn."

The top? Who and where was the top? Was this not New York? Where all the best of the best ended up?

"Go see this guy I know in Colorado," he instructed. "He's the best."

THE BEST... These words sent my typical Type A, must-succeed-at-all-costs young professional genes into a frenzy. I went to find this guru on the internet.

I scrolled down the plethora of classes and clinics offered... Oooo, who knew there were so many? But my focus was intent... Get with the guru... the best... the top – The Man.

So, I signed up and off I went to Colorado – home of beautiful Aspen trees, never-ending blue skies, mountains that people sang about, horses, and the horse men and women who rode them. Off to The Man, who would teach me how to ride.

I showed up at this great place – no cars, people galloping around bareback… dust… cowboys… awesome.

I tripped lightly across the wooden porch and found myself a seat in the – yep, you guessed it – horseshoe. I was at the end. I surveyed my fellow horse men and women. Wow… they looked like, well, horse men and women… hats, boots, chaps. I sneaked a peek at my boots, bought ten years earlier in Texas, and breathed a small sigh of relief that I had done so. They looked worn and broken in. A clever disguise.

Suddenly, there was a shift in the air. People stirred and sat up straighter, and all of a sudden, there he was – this big, handsome, Marlboro-man cowboy straight out of central casting. I mean, this was better than I could have imagined.

His energy commanded the room. He started at the opposite end of the horseshoe, asking questions about who everyone was and why we were there.

"Hi, my name is Bob from Montana and I have 20 horses and I'm here with one of them because he doesn't trailer load." (Whatever that was.)

"Hi, my name is Jane from Wyoming and I have 100 horses and I'm here to learn how to be lighter." (Judging the distance from the cabins to the lodge, this would not take long.)

"I'm Sandy from Texas and I have a million horses…"

I was beginning to panic.

Finally I felt his intense gaze upon me.

I swallowed and launched into it.

"Hi, my name is Lisa and I'm from New York."

"New York?" he said kindly. I relaxed just a bit. "Upstate New York?" he surmised. "Where?"

"Oh, no," I corrected. "Manhattan."

There was a slight pause.

"Manhattan? Where do you keep your horse in Manhattan?"

"Oh, I don't have a horse."

This actually stopped him. His and all other eyes were upon me. I was wondering if the power of thought was strong enough to make me evaporate at this point.

"You don't have a horse." A statement. Not a question. "Lisa from New York, why are you here?"

Oh… phew. I could answer this… "Because I want to learn how to ride and I was told you were the best."

I said this genuinely and I think this might actually have saved me from being handed a refund and being asked to leave. He turned his gaze back to the group and I felt like someone had unplugged me. I sagged back into the chair. The worst was over – or so I thought.

"OK," he said. "Here's what we are going to do… Get your horses, saddle up, and meet me in the main arena in 15 minutes."

Saddle up? What the hell did that mean? Wasn't one of those cowboys going to bring me my mount all saddled and ready to go in the front of the lodge, like in those resort brochures?

"Ummmm, excuse me sir?"

He turned around. "Yes, Lisa from New York. What can I help you with?"

"Ummmm… I don't have a horse, as I mentioned, *or* a saddle."

"It's OK. Just go out into the corral and your horse will find you. Oh, and someone will drop a saddle off at the tack room." And off he strode.

I stood there for a minute. Then I realized what he had said.

My horse will find *me?* What kind of cowboy hooey was *that?*

Not knowing what else to do, I mustered up my best swagger and strode off into the direction of what I thought was a corral. I went to the gate and was greeted by hundreds of horse faces. Every time I tried to open the gate, they crowded around pushing and shoving and snorting, and they were *much* bigger than me.

So, I rethought my entrance strategy, climbed over the fence, and jumped into the middle of the sea of horses. I felt very athletic… and cowgirl like. This wasn't so bad. I strode around myself a bit, starting to enjoy this swagger thing.

My horse will find me. Sure. I ignored the very first thing I was told to do and started perusing all the wonderful creatures in front of me. And there he was – a beautiful paint standing just off to the side. He turned his head and looked at me. Well, that was a signal if ever I saw one. Just as I was about to approach my fine steed, I felt a nudge from behind.

I turned and looked at this short, fat, brown horse close enough to me that as she took a deep breath in, it felt like she would suck my face off my head.

What was this? No way. This was not my horse.

I shrugged her off and took off in the direction of the paint. The paint turned and walked away from me, and the little brown horse turned and followed me. I followed the paint; the brown horse followed me. As I sped up, so did the paint and the brown horse. Soon we were all running in a circle around the edge of the corral with the other horses watching in amusement from the center.

Wait I minute! This was not very becoming. I stopped. The paint slowed down, but kept walking away. I felt a nudge from behind. I turned, and the short, fat, brown horse put her nose in my armpit and nuzzled me.

Your horse will find you.

This was my horse. Wow. *This* was my horse?

I wasn't sure how I felt. Well that's not true. I knew exactly how I felt. I felt uncomfortable. I stared back at the little brown horse standing quietly next to me, staring back.

She took a deep breath and let out a big sigh. I knew how she felt.

I lassoed this wild Mustang-type beast next to me with a rope thing that I sort of tied in a knot around her neck and headed off to where my fellow horse men and women were gathered around a tack shed. As I approached with my trusty horse in hand, all proud and everything, they headed out, en masse, leaving behind a cloud of dust and one lone little saddle.

I looked at it and then back to the horse and then back to it…

"OK," I thought. "How hard can this be?"

I bent over to pick up the saddle, and almost fell on my face. This thing weighed like a gazillion pounds. I looked around for help, but all of a sudden the very busy ranch seemed devoid of people. I distinctly remember seeing friendly-looking cowboys in the brochure. Where the #%$%^$ were they?

I took a breath… I could do this. I picked up the saddle so it was held underside out and perpendicular toward the horse. Somehow I managed to get it to sort of shoulder height with my knees buckled under me. Conk… I struck her right in the side, then I sort of pushed the saddle up from there. But apparently, I pushed a little too hard and it went sliding off the other side. In hindsight, I can appreciate what a good and patient horse this was. At the time, I thought it was normal that horses stood still while humans belabored them with saddlery.

I ran around to the other side and once again did the lift and slide upward technique of saddling my horse. This time, I managed to actually get it up and on her back. And it stayed there… Great.

Then I pondered what to do with all these strap things hanging down everywhere. I stuck my head under her belly to see if there was something to attach it to under there…

"Hi," I heard a voice from above.

I popped my head out from below and saw – thank goodness – a cowboy person.

"You may not want to stick your head under a horse's belly," he stated simply.

"Oh, really? Well... ummm... Can you tell me how to attach the saddle?"

"Sure." And with a flip and a zip and turning the horse back and forth at lightning speed, lo and behold, the saddle was on. He continued to untangled my brilliant knots around her neck and did some more rope magic... and poof... reins!

This guy was great. He handed me the reins, smiled, and rode off into the sunset... or at least... away.

I stared at the horse. She looked properly outfitted...

She stared at me...

"Don't look at me," I thought. "I don't know *what* I'm doing."

I stuck my foot in the stirrup and pulled myself up. The saddle slid toward me. Hmmm... Oh well... I guess this was... natural.

Off I went in the direction of the main arena at a sort of 45-degree angle to my horse.

The next day, as we were being filled in on the day's events, beautiful dark clouds began to roll in. Oh yes, God does love me. Nap time provided by Yours Truly in the form of a rainstorm.

I sat back and waited to be dismissed.

The Man sort of looked up briefly and without any concern, continued.

"So let's saddle up and be ready to go as soon as possible before the rain starts."

What a silly exercise. Saddle up, and then what? When it starts to rain, unsaddle up? Oh well, I guess this was all part of the experience.

So, off I went to once again torture my horse with the tacking up.

Some time later, sweating from head to toe, I managed to drag my horse back to where my teacher was just finishing up the lesson for the morning.

A loud crack overhead gave us fair warning that the storm was about to commence.

"OK, take a break and meet back here in ten minutes."

I stood there realizing slowly that not only was I *not* going to get praise and recognition for getting the saddle on myself (now hanging at a sort of 32-degree angle, a vast improvement), but, I realized we were going to ride in the rain.

As a divine answer, a very large heavy raindrop hit me in the eye. Followed by another… and another.

Thankfully, I had been warned by my first teacher to bring some rain boots and a raincoat. I left my horse and ran in to get my gear. By the time I came back out the heavens had opened. My class had gone to stand in a nearby covered arena.

There was my horse, still standing where I left her, looking like a drowned rat. Apparently, it is an unwritten cowboy rule that you do not touch another man's horse.

I dragged my soggy mare to the coverall, where I announced that in the future it would be fine to touch my mount. As I was dabbing very ineffectively to try to dry off my leather saddle with a small and tiny Kleenex, my fellow cowpokes were trying really hard not to laugh. It was about this time that our great leader went riding by. He glanced over briefly as he rode by like a war hero on his fiery black steed. Then he stopped. He backed his horse up – really, he sort of glided backwards… I couldn't even get mine to go forward without looking drunk – anyway, he eased back until he was directly opposite me. He looked down at my rubber-clad feet.

Now, the boots I brought with me were my cute little Miu Miu's. I thought the orange added a nice accent of color to the brown, muddy surroundings.

All of a sudden everyone else was staring at them… intently. How did my boots become the focal point of the class?

"Nice boots," he said, and rode on. I knew it was not a compliment.

I sighed, standing in the mud with my now very silly orange boots, wondering what the hell I was doing here. I mean, who was I kidding? I would never learn how to ride. I couldn't even get the boots straight.

At this moment, my little mare came up behind me and nudged me. I gave her a hug around her very wet neck and said, "Come on." And we walked off. She just followed me. I was so distracted and humiliated by my lack of cowboy fashion sense that I did not clutch the halter rope and drag my horse behind me. She just walked on her own quietly beside me all the way across the ranch.

The Man rode by me again. I did my best to be invisible and to cover my boots with the mud I was sloshing through.

"Hey Lisa. That's pretty fancy stuff." He smiled and rode on.

What did he say? I felt his compliment was sincere, but had no idea what fancy thing he noticed, as my boots were clearly not in the running.

I found out much later that walking around with your horse beside you with nothing attaching the two of you was called being at liberty. Great horse men and horse women study the art of being at liberty as a lifelong pursuit and the ultimate reflection of horse mastery.

I seemed to have achieved it unwittingly. Of course, once I knew how desirable it was to achieve it, I became determined to have it. And in doing so, I lost it. As I grasped this, I took my first tiny step across the bridge of unconsciousness into the land of presence.

It seemed the more I became educated in horsemanship, the less I knew. I had come from a world where, when I strived to achieve, I was met with success. Here, it seemed the harder I reached for it, the more it eluded me. As I sat and did nothing, success couldn't get close to me fast enough. My horse showed up, and stuck around. Not only did she stick around, she followed me around happily.

It was weird. When I didn't think about it happening, it happened. The minute I thought about it, my horse left.

Bingo. The key to connection: Stay in head… stay stuck; drop into heart… transformational connection.

Somehow, all alone in this dirt and mud and jingling and jangling of horses and horse men and women, I found my horse. Or she found me. And somehow, in finding my horse, I found my heart. There it was, in all its glory, just hanging out where I left it so many years ago. And she put her soft little nose right on it. And breathed life into it again.

Every day brought new insights. Sometimes she would snort at what I was telling her, as if she couldn't believe her ears. Sometimes she would nuzzle me gently when she uncovered those tender bits I had tucked away. And sometimes we didn't talk at all. We just hung out. She would graze quietly next to me as I lay in the tall grass and watched the sky pass by. But whatever the moment was, it felt real… and fantastic. I liked it. I felt alive. I could feel what it was like to just be me. I was indeed having the ride of my life. And it had little to do with getting on the back of a horse.

This was indeed liberty… the freedom that comes from being real.

My horse found me when I was so numb that I did not know I was lost. She very gently carried me back to the land of living and the richness and fullness that comes with being there.

Slowly, as I recognized what she had done for me, I fell head over heels in love with my heart. For the first time in my life, I recognized its strength. I appreciated its courage. And, just like what my horse had shown me about being at liberty, my heart led me, not by tying me down and forcing me to be with it. It took the lead simply by loving me unconditionally and wanting all of me to show up. And when I did, when every last bit of me finally showed up, the noise stopped and I could hear clearly. I could hear my heart and its great wisdom. I could hear the call of my nature, and my purpose and place in it. It was calling me home. And once I could hear it, I knew I was not lost anymore.

Somewhere in being a nobody in this strange new world of horses, I became a somebody to myself. A real somebody. Not a façade. Just a person. No frills. No extras. I found me reflected back through the eyes of a trusting, loving horse who saw the real me. Not the person who was trying so hard to be someone so she could be loved. She saw the person who was already lovable, just as she was right in that moment. And that was enough for her. She loved me unconditionally.

Eventually, I had to say goodbye to this great creature who had brought me so far in such a short space of time. I took my last walk into the mare pasture to see her. As always, she lifted her head and nickered a soft welcome as I approached. The lump in my throat was like a piece of porous volcanic rock – hard and scratchy. The tears that had filled my eyes blurred the picture of her before me, their heat hot on my skin as they spilled over onto my cheeks. How could I leave her? She was a part of me. And had a part of me.

She came toward me with her head lowered, nickering quietly, her soft lips nuzzling me as she searched for a cookie. We stood together as she quietly savored the found treat, completely present to each other in these final moments.

I gave her one last hug before I turned and walked away. She walked with me to the gate. This was more than liberty. This was heartfelt connection. What I had learned is that when there is heartfelt connection, liberty happens.

I stood at the gate, unable to tear myself away, so she once again filled in for me where I was lacking. She reached over the fence one last time, nuzzled my ear, and then turned and walked away, not looking back, taking all of her, and a part of me, back to the herd.

I left Manhattan, home of Miu Mius and many misguided perceptions. I let my heart, not my head, take the lead and when I did, my fantasy of living a good, simple life became a real living dream. I moved out of my New York apartment and moved into my heart. It led me on the most unexpected journey. I now live north of a little town in Colorado, with my horses. I tell my story to those who want to know it, and share the horses with others who are searching for that missing piece in themselves.

Many people ask how I left all that I knew, all that supposed security, and move west to immerse myself in all I did not know. Many ask, "Was I scared?"

The answer is yes. But I was more scared of living a life that I would one day regret. A life that I would look back on and know in my heart that I had not lived to its fullest, that I had left the richness of it somewhere on some corporate conference table. That to me was much scarier than venturing into this unknown. I was scared of staying the person I had become, because deep down, that mare had shown me it was not who I really was.

How did I make the leap?

I didn't leap. I climbed on the back of a great horse and let her carry me. And carry me she did, across that silly bridge that I had been too scared to cross before by myself.

She is still my greatest teacher.

There was no way I could leave her in that pasture. She had healed and filled my heart. And that does not happen every day.

I left the mare pasture but I did not leave the grounds. I went to the office and found the owner of the establishment.

"I need to ask you a question," I blurted out.

He looked up kindly and cocked his head as he sat back, awaiting my question.

"I really love that horse and I am not sure if it is because she is my first horse or because she is a really good horse. Can you tell me which it is?"

He lowered his gaze and contemplated his fingertips for a long silence before he looked up at me with a smile that spoke to my heart.

"It's both," he said. "She is your first horse and there is nothing like that – ever. And yes, she is a really good horse, too."

I did not know what I was doing, but I knew enough at this time not to question what was coming up loud and clear from deep inside me. I said, "I want to take her home with me."

His smile deepened and his eyes looked through mine all the way into my soul.

"I am not in the habit of selling my horses."

"I know I don't know much right now, but I am very smart and I can learn."

He looked down again at his fingertips.

My heart was pounding as this man held a piece of it in his hands.

Finally, he looked up.

"Did you know that I saw you both every morning?"

My jaw dropped.

"I watched you in the arena every morning when you snuck in at 4 a.m. I watched you getting bounced around morning after morning. You never gave up. Neither did she. She kept bouncing you around until you got it. And you did. That little mare has taught some of my best instructors and hundreds of students. I will miss her."

And with that he stood up, shook my hand, and said, "Take good care of her."

I stood there. My heart seemed not to be able to contain the emotion that drove it upward into my throat and pushed its way alongside of the lump that was already there, almost preventing me from taking the breath that I needed to whisper, "Thank you."

I had no idea the journey I had just embarked upon.

We left the ranch together. I had to learn quickly. We only had each other to rely on. I trusted her immediately as a reliable source. But I had to reach deep to trust myself as one. Each time I did reach, my confidence grew. And in that confidence, and in that reliance, we learned a deep trust. And in that trust we gained a profound love and connection.

Both of us were workhorses in our own respective arenas. Both of us left behind our herds as we crossed the bridge over the river of the unknown to get to the other side.

I have been asked, "What was that like when you got to the other side?"

My answer? I don't know. I did not get there. And I am not sure I ever will. Another bridge always seems to present itself, with an invitation to cross, and a choice whether to do so or not – to cross even deeper into another unknown land.

And when life does throw me an unexpected curve that knocks me off track, it's nice to know I can simply hang back in the herd and follow for a while. The horses always seem to know where the path is.

Master horse men and women ask a question as they study and teach being at liberty: "If your horse had a choice, would it choose to be with you?"

I took this question to heart – the place where I keep all things precious – and take it out every now and again and look at it. My horse is now my mirror, every minute of every day. If ever I lose the sense of who I am, my horse is right there to show me.

Miss Hakomi Banks, my little brown horse, transformed into a beautiful sorrel mare.

I wonder what she sees I have become?

Photo by Jamie Wiliams

Miss Hakomi Banks

I would like to thank my beloved fiancé, Jess, whose continued support and belief in me makes all of this possible, and even more wonderful. Thank you for loving me, for loving our land, and for loving our horses.

About
Lisa Dee

Lisa Dee is the creator and guide of Equist™, a groundbreaking process that puts people back in touch with their instinctual selves and their own source of power. Through this clear and focused process her clients let go of the limiting beliefs, patterns, and relationships that hold them back from achieving what they desire in their lives. In doing so, they reach their greatest potential. The result of the work is profound and permanent change. Clients gain the ability to see themselves in a positive new light that illuminates their true self, their true purpose, and their place in life. This process gives people clarity, bringing people to the place where they connect with the power of their instincts and their true nature. The sustainability of the process ripples through every aspect of their lives.

Lisa's ranch, Vista Caballo, is an exclusive equine experiential center based in Dove Creek, Colorado, and is dedicated to self awareness, the development of human potential, and personal growth.

Passionate and devoted to her studies, Lisa has trained for years in Equine Experiential Learning, energy medicine, and natural horsemanship. Lisa continues her studies with the best "whisperers" in the country, looking to further her understanding of and connection to her horses and energy healing to the benefit of her clients. As always, her horses remain her best and favorite teachers.

A highly successful entrepreneur, Lisa founded and operated two multi-million dollar businesses simultaneously for over fifteen years before she started Vista Caballo. She has been a guest speaker at Columbia University's School for New Ventures and was voted Woman of The Year in 2008 in Personal Development by NAPEW.

Lisa can be reached at ld@vistacaballo.com. Visit her website at www.vistacaballo.com.

When Love Comes To Call

By Karen Head

There are six horses in my barn tonight. It is winter; the ground is frozen solid, and snow is on the way. In the evenings I clean stalls to keep the horses comfortable and feed hay to keep them warm. I wield the pitchfork around their legs, tossing manure in a bucket across the stall. The horses remain calm. They trust me, pitchfork and all. Most nights, Ceili, my big heart horse, will reach around to nuzzle me as I clean his stall. In this moment I am at peace with the world.

Ceili came to me ten years ago as a gangly two year-old. His owner did not like his conformation. He had a huge head and a skinny neck. I wasn't sure about my own ability to handle a two year-old. It had been years since I had ridden a young horse. Who was I to take on a Clydesdale/Thoroughbred cross? I was a middle-aged woman with teenage children and many years since I had trained horses. From childhood, I had been deeply connected to horses, but taking on a two year-old was daunting.

The angels in my life started to work hard for me at this point. Mark, my sweetheart, encouraged me to take a chance, to buy Ceili. He honored the love I felt for horses and it was from this place that he encouraged me. He joined the people in my life who led me to horses and thus to myself. I needed support for a little while as I stepped out of my old beliefs that I was inadequate and too old to change.

Ceili has grown into a magnificent horse both in conformation and character. I did train him myself. His gentle spirit met with my courage and we became a team. Training him gave me reason to believe in myself. I broke out of my own limiting beliefs, followed my passion, and began a new career. Ceili joined Pony, Ernest, and Kelly, horses that, in my lifetime, opened my heart when it was locked and closed to any possibility of me making a difference in the world.

But I began at the end and have traveled to the middle of my story without telling you my beginning. This is how my story must be told for to know what horses teach, we must follow their lead and become nomads. Just as wild horses travel over hundreds of miles grazing on various grasses and plants, I travel through memories offering what comes to me in the moment, trusting that each recollection nourishes my story. Cleaning stalls on cold winter nights and running an equine-facilitated learning center is my present. My past is full of horses and people who taught me to believe in myself and to claim my place on this planet.

My life with horses began on Christmas day, 1960. I was five years old when my parents gave me Pony. Everything was big when I was five; it was a mile to the front door from the staircase and down the stairs to Big Frank, who was holding Pony for me. In my eyes, that little yellow pony was perfect.

Frank said, "This is your pony," and that is how my first horse got his name. Frank was gigantic, his skin a beautiful deep brown, except for his hands; they were very black from working a lifetime in the sun. His arms were the size of tree trunks. He would hold out his arm for me to swing on and could easily toss me on top of any horse. I loved him without reservation.

Frank was the first dependable man in my life. He had no formal education, signed his name with an X, and knew more about loving a little girl than anyone I have ever known. He was there when I first rode a horse. He made certain Pony would be safe for a five-year-old tomboy with little or no sense. He drove me to school on time every morning and home again in the afternoon to ride Pony. I always felt at home in the barn and with him.

He had started as a stable boy when he was in the second grade. At seven years old, he worked full days carrying water and cleaning stalls. He knew the hard side of life. To me, he was always a happy man. The despair of living a harsh life wasn't what he taught me. He taught me about my potential by teaching me how to ride, to drive a jeep when I had to stand up to push in the clutch, and to take care of a horse. He was always just as happy to see me as I was to see him. Frank Taylor was a wise man.

My father was also wise, but in a very different way than Frank. He had many college degrees and was an accomplished entrepreneur. He was just a few years old when he refused his father's name, Earl. He ran away on his little toddler legs if anyone called him Earl. At fifteen years-old, my father ran down the dirt road that headed east out of Trinity, Texas. He left behind a town too small to hide from the shame Earl heaped on his proud teenage son while lying drunk in the streets begging for kindness. Dad finally stopped running away from Earl the night he died.

My father ran over his mother, his children, his wife, and anyone whom he perceived to block his path. He ran over women by the dozens and never stopped to feel the loneliness in his wake.

I was four years old when we moved to our farm in Virginia. I could hop stones across creeks, be daring and climb rock faced slopes. I could be outside all day long. In the house, bumping into my family was painful and degrading.

Even though my father left Texas far behind him, Earl came to live with us. No one ever spoke his name. We children didn't even know he existed. Nonetheless, Earl might as well have been passing out on our kitchen table every night because Dad never felt completely safe; not in his own home or his own skin. He wasn't safe with two medical degrees so he earned a law degree, but he wasn't safe with that either so he became a professor. And he ran to achieve more, build more buildings, and more businesses. My father taught all of us to run. My mother ran to the city and my sister and brother ran to excel in school, sports, and music. I ran out of the house and down the driveway to the barn, to the horses, and to Big Frank.

Big Frank had a reputation as a problem drinker when he came to work for my father. My parents were told that he wasn't to be trusted, but my mother thought outside that box and trusted him anyway. My mother lived in my father's shadow. Yet there were crucial times when her light would shine through. She insisted that Frank have a clean, dry, home. He was taking care of her children and he needed a home. So Frank came to live in the new apartment in our barn.

Frank used to tell me that he had a sister named Rose and he had to see her by six every night or she would be angry with him. I of course understood this, having a big sister myself who barely tolerated my existence much less my exuberance. (Rose was really his girlfriend, I found out many years later.) Big Frank would shoo me home at 5:00 every night with stories of scary animals living in the woods between the barn and our house. He would lift me up and over the railings and then I would run home faster than any ole lion could catch me; long before it got really dark when monsters would come out of the woods of Virginia looking for little girls to eat.

We kids moved into the city with my mother when I was eleven, leaving my father at the farm. I could only go to the farm on weekends.

In the city, the monsters didn't live in the woods; the monsters lived in my new classroom. I was lost in a class with 30 children. In one night I went from an easy farm life to struggling for acceptance in a city school and confined to a fenced back yard every afternoon. Frank wasn't there to drive me anywhere; I rode the bus, learning the rules from crossing guards and curt bus drivers. There were cool clothes, cool people, cool music, none of which I understood.

I was totally preoccupied with surviving in this city school when I was told that Big Frank was gone for good. It seems that Frank just couldn't make it to work on time some mornings and when he started missing work for entire days my father had to let him go. Big Frank had driven me to school from Kindergarten through the fifth grade and he was never, not one time, late. How could he have changed so much in a few months?

I felt powerless and no one noticed my sorrow – not even me; we were all too busy running.

I had lost my best friend and closest ally and I was too young to understand that Frank kept his drinking at bay because of the love he shared with a little girl who needed him. I only knew that he was gone and the apartment where he lived was empty. I found solace with the horses.

Both of my siblings excelled in the city schools, taking after our parents. School was my constant challenge and I was a disappointment to my entire family. No one knew about dyslexia then, so my inability to read words or numbers was chalked up to laziness. In the light of my family's academic prowess, of course I would have appeared glaringly inept. This was how I was treated; I was pigeonholed in these big schools, branded, and put in my place.

Losing Big Frank should have been the most devastating moment of my young life, but truth be told, moving to a big city school devastated me every day of the week. Having the horses on weekends carried me though my school week. I transferred the love and safety I felt with Big Frank to the horses. Big Frank became a nice memory.

Frank died a couple of years after he left the farm. I never told him goodbye or thanked him for loving me and protecting my young spirit.

He was in my heart last year when I drove to Kentucky and rescued a yearling Thoroughbred who was to be euthanized. He has a breathing problem that prohibits him from running races. I named him, B.F. Taylor, after one of the finest men I will ever know.

Taylor started off with fear in his eyes and panic deep in his soul, having experienced mostly rough handling through many medical procedures.

He was rejected and tossed aside, branded as unworthy of respect or concern. I have loved him through this, just the way Big Frank loved me. I believed that he would learn to trust people, that he would discover a new purpose, other than racing, and that he could achieve the greatness that his ancestors knew. This young horse brought me to a higher level of acceptance of love's power and myself. Taylor has taught me to act on my beliefs, to shine through fear's shadow with conviction that love will serve a higher need.

Believing in love is often easier to say than to put into daily practice. Taylor scared people on my farm. They believed he would always be untrustworthy. He had colic one night and wouldn't let anyone near him as he hurled himself against the fence. He was trying to ease his pain while he tore his shoulder wide open. I realized that Taylor would have to decide if he were going to live or die. With that understanding between us, Taylor stopped his frantic self-destruction, allowed himself to be caught, and his colic cleared up. From that moment on he has never panicked and threatened another person; we all trust him now. I questioned my decision to work with this troubled horse many times over the months prior to his colic, but I kept returning to love. Loving Taylor gave him a second chance. He will grow to be a fine horse. He has a gentle spirit, just like his namesake.

Learning to trust love took root on that chilly Christmas morning, when I raced out of the house with no coat on and felt the warmth of joy spread through me as I reached out to touch Pony. I knew for certain that I was safe with him and that I was going to be his girl.

What happened to the confidence I felt on that frigid Christmas morning? By the time I was in sixth grade I had lost any belief I had in myself in all arenas of life but one. I always felt comfortable with my horses. I remember the certain knowing I had with Pony; wherever we went together, I was safe on him with or without a saddle. I could go across streams, logs, and sticky mud holes with no doubts. More importantly, I knew to turn around if Pony felt afraid. I relied on my intuition to stay safe with Pony. Yet I couldn't navigate my way through the cafeteria at my new school, and froze in class if asked a question. I was lost with no one to depend on.

My father bought Kelly when I had outgrown Pony. Kelly was a sweet-natured, smooth-cantering buckskin quarter horse who, like Pony, lived out his life on the farm. We rode across the rough terrain of junior high school together. I could go anywhere on Kelly, and often did. I rode him into a country store, the main lobby of the conference center, on icy lakes, and on all-day rides past abandoned homes with slave quarters and summer kitchens.

After I lost Frank, Kelly gently carried me into confidence and I learned to trust myself again. Cantering on him was so easy. I knew that he made me look good and I treasured that. To a 13-year-old girl, looking good is tantamount to survival. So, looking good cantering on Kelly gave me the feeling of being admired, even if it was just the two of us loping across a back field of the farm. I knew we were beautiful. I could feel it.

By the time I was in high school, my grades were horrible and my social standing even worse. I truly hated gym class, basketball being the worst and most degrading experience. No one missed me when I disappeared behind the stage curtain after role call. One day, behind this curtain, I met Susie and my school life changed. Susie was a cheerleader, the homecoming princess, and was the most popular girl I had ever been near enough to speak to. There she was, sitting on stage during gym biting her nails, and wide-eyed when I dove behind the curtain. We started to talk. I didn't know any boy stories, didn't know any of her friends, but I could talk about one thing with confidence – horses.

Susie loved horses. Her father's name was Phillip, which, as she told me, meant lover of horses. We became friends behind that curtain, much to my astonishment. Our love of horses prevented us from inflicting the cruel social conditions held by high school students.

Susie came out to the farm for many weekends and we would ride all day long. With Susie, I found a place in high school that was far from my special education rooms and degrading exchanges in the hallway. Susie was my ticket to "normal," and she found her escape too. It seems that being popular demanded trade-offs. Susie, at 13, had been expected to be sexy, use drugs, and act cool doing all of this. With me, Susie was able to reclaim some childhood time. As we rode, we shared stories of all the families in the abandoned houses and then began to make up dreams for our future together. We were going to adopt 13 children and have a bathroom with two showers and a huge toothbrush rack. We rode together into a lifelong friendship, accepting each other for who we were, rather than trying to be what everyone else expected us to be.

Susie rode Kelly and I started to ride Ernest. Ernest wasn't easy like Kelly; he would shy and bolt at the very littlest of things. He had kicked one whole side of his stall to shreds when he first came to the farm. Ernest was a full brother to the seven time grand champion American Saddlebred mare, My My. But Ernest, like me, didn't display any family tendencies for high standing in competitions, so he came to live at the farm.

Ernest and I bloomed together. His high fright response matched my own. We did well together. I knew when he was about to blow and could ride him through his bucking, rearing, and bolting. He swam in the lake with me, played tag in the moonlight with Susie riding Kelly, and absorbed my teenage-sized emotions, returning only love. I said lightly for years that Ernest saved my teenage butt. Now I understand the weight of this statement. As a teenager, I couldn't express any emotion in my family or in school, so Ernest basically got it all – the confusion of living in the city with my absent mother, the anger over my powerless life with my father, and the despair over failing again and again in school. He also held the passionate, devoted love I was filled with for my horses and the land.

Ernest lived until he was thirty, long after Susie and I had gone off to college together, were each other's maids of honor, and godmothers to each other's children. We never lived in the big house with 13 children, but we've always stayed close to each other's hearts.

I would bring my children to Virginia several times a year to visit my father. I didn't always get to visit with Ernest, but one November visit I insisted on seeing him. I walked out to the field by myself. He was standing on a knoll swaying with weakness. I walked up to him and put my hand on his neck, telling him how much I loved him and how much I had missed him. Before leaving the farm, I asked that he be put down because he was so very weak. Winter was coming on and he needn't feel the chill in his bones any longer. That evening, Ernest went to the spot where he was to be buried and lay down to die.

Like my delayed response to Big Frank, I didn't feel the extent of the gifts Ernest had given me until much later. Ernest gave me sparkle and pizzazz, he gave me time to think and time to pay close attention. He gave me reason to believe in myself. I knew that if I could ride Ernest, I could do anything I set my mind to. This led me to develop skills to cope with school. I began to challenge myself to ride through school.

Ernest taught me that courage comes from inside. I became the leader and he my willing partner. We danced together until I grew up and left home. Yet he waited for me to say goodbye, calling me to him, asking me to remember my courage and my ability to meet a challenge head on.

My father died almost 10 years later. He had been a powerful, though difficult force in my life. Losing him was the beginning of a sea change, one that led me back to horses.

I stayed by my father's side while he maneuvered his way through tests, chemotherapy, and radiation. It was grace that led me to forgiveness and peace with my father. Even into adulthood, his sarcasm kept me quiet and small. Like my mother's conviction about Big Frank those many years earlier, I knew that being with my father was the right thing to do. I left my family and new horses in Indiana to go to Virginia every other week for months.

As a child, I knew Dad had given me horses and had hired people to take care of them and paid the expenses. I loved my father for this gift. That thread of love… the tiny cobweb strand of love… was there waiting to wrap around the two of us at the end of his life. My father and I are connected forever, not by fear and anger, but by love. At the end of Dad's life as he expressed his love for me, I learned that my extraordinary father was proud of me. This was enough.

After my father's funeral I went back to Indiana and focused on my new horses. Over the years of lessons at a riding academy, I had been trained to be dominant over horses, to show them who was boss. Toby, a palomino quarter horse, offered enough challenges to this belief that I had to ask for help. Toby taught me that force was ineffective. All I was doing was adding stress and anxiety to both our lives. Once I was introduced to a gentle way of handling Toby, all the years of riding with the wind on Pony, Kelly, and Ernest came home to my heart. I began to trust myself, and then Toby and I started to understand each other. He was my rock when my marriage began to crumble.

Toby was constant, a steady partner during this time of change. For two years he was the gold ring I would reach for as I went round and round on the merry-go-round of divorce, insanity, and despair. Toby taught me to pick my head up despite a failed marriage. He insisted that I look ahead, eyes forward to see life ahead of me, not downcast and beaten. We both learned to slow down together and to enjoy the ride. He stayed in Indiana when I moved to a city in North Carolina and thought that my time with horses was over. I miss Toby every day of the world, but as we learned together, sometimes the best thing to do is to let go of a tight rein.

My story is intrinsically tied to horses. Being with horses touches my spirit and I feel love. This love gathered together pieces of me that have been fragmented by casual neglect and cruel words. This is an essential aspect of who I have become. I know that people do the best that they can. Earl, my father, Big Frank – all did the absolute best that they could do.

With my horses I learned to love in the wide open. What would my life have been like without horses? I can't know this. All I know is that being unwanted by some people isn't a definition of who I am. It is an example of how people can be blinded with limiting beliefs – seeing only a racehorse that can't run, or a young Clydesdale cross with a skinny neck, or a little girl who can't read. There were people and horses in my life who could see past labels and limitations. Through patience and understanding they showed me my strength – my light.

Being with horses taught me to lift my head, be aware of my surroundings, resist dominance, embrace my power, and to run down the stairs and out the door whenever love comes to call. I remember this on cold winter nights as Ceili reaches out to nuzzle me while I clean his stall. I learned it a long time ago, one winter morning when love came in the guise of a large black man in a jaunty wool cap holding a scruffy little pony.

Photo by Barnwell Photography

Ceili

I am grateful to my children, my partner, my family, my teachers, and my horses. Each one is a blessing and support in my work.

About Karen Head

I was raised with horses in my back yard where I could catch them, groom them, and take off riding for the entire day. My mother rode in horse shows all across the country. When she was a teen, she would arrive at the stables and her horse would be groomed, tacked up, and ready to ride. She never groomed a horse. My mother gave me the opportunity to do that for myself.

I always knew where to look to find my father. He used to tell me, "You know where I am, Kare, if you need me." My father could not depend on his father, so when he built a home he stayed there. He was easy to find. Both of my parents offered me what they most wanted from their childhood, but never had.

My life has reflected the free spirit and innocent passion of the sixties. I was lucky to grow up during that time. Although there were the devastating moments – assassinations, unresolved war, and terrible conflicts in America – my life was teeming with passion, purpose, and challenge. I met Dr. King. I went to peace marches in Washington, D.C. I knew Nixon was guilty. I sang folk songs and loved the Beatles. I went to college and studied horse care, horsemanship, horse breeding and genetics, and theatre arts. I loved teaching and couldn't tolerate the confinements of a public school classroom, so I started a theatre program for children. In graduate school I studied ways to teach people using the arts to enhance education. Many teachers have changed the course of my life. Linda Kohanov and Kathleen Barry Ingram are two of these teachers. They offered a way to honor how horses illuminate the strengths and talents people bring to the world. My children have been my teachers, helping me to let go of rigidity and enjoy them as they took root in their lives as loving and talented adults. Mark, my partner, has moved three times with me, while I searched for just the right place to build my business. We live on 112 acres now, a beautiful spot in the mountains of North Carolina. Here, with the help of the horses, people remember themselves and the gifts they bring to life.

I have so many gifts, so many people to bow down to in respect and gratitude. I am blessed to live here on my farm. I'm settled now, with nine horses. I've returned to a life with passion, purpose, and challenge. Through my work I express my passion for the land and horses, I am dedicated to helping people remember their truth and strength, and I am reminded every day to do what the horses teach – open my heart and find contentment in the simple pleasures.

For more information, visit www.equinection.org.

The Horses Are Calling...

By Susan Williams

It was a warm, sunny spring afternoon in the mountains of Colorado when I loaded up my camera gear, hopped into my car, and drove to town to see the Mustang adoption day at the county fairgrounds. Although the sun was shining, it was not a friendly sun for photography, but instead was cold and harsh. That was of little concern to me. I am always open to what gifts the universe has waiting for me, since much of the magical and ethereal quality of my photography happens after I have taken the imagery. My desire to go to the adoption was triggered by witnessing and experiencing a couple of epic equine events only a few weeks earlier.

The first event was an opportunity to photograph the largest horse roundup in the nation, located a short four hour drive from home. Never having visited northwestern Colorado, I was excited about the thought of an adventure.

My main motivation for the trek was for more horse imagery for a contemplative self-portrait series called Windhorse, a collection of images where the horse reflects back to us our true nature. A Tibetan allegory, it represents the strength of the human soul, with two components: the first being the wind, or chi, the equivalent of our life force energy or vitality, and secondly, the horse, which symbolizes strength and the ability to overcome life's obstacles. Windhorses bring with them an ancient truth and deep spiritual awareness, and by connecting to this inner wisdom of the horse, we can come to intimately know ourselves. The imagery I was hoping to capture would reflect this learning.

The annual spring roundup was a time for the ranch to bring in their herd from their thawing winter wonderland. At least one hundred photographers had gathered for the event and the air was charged with energy as we all waited for the arrival of the horses with the excitement and anticipation of small children. It was an amazing and epic sight to witness several hundred horses galloping in off the range, guided by the skilled ranch hands. I could hear and feel the ground rumbling well before I could see the horses. Thundering hooves announced the arrival of the horses, dust everywhere, their heads tossing, accompanied with lots of whinnying. Any one of us could have been trampled at any given moment as the horses ran circles around us, yet we all stood transfixed, cameras glued to our faces, shutters clicking. I didn't know which way to turn as the horses rapidly enveloped me. These horses knew their routine well and seemed to enjoy it as much as I was. I felt the archetypal energy and spirit of the individual horses, as well as the herd.

Electing to follow behind the herd, to feel the collective energy of the group as they rumbled past, I wondered if the friend who had accompanied me and I were destined to be at the rear of the herd for the rest of the day. What a pleasant surprise when some cowgirls positioned their horses in front of the vehicle and parted the herd, waving us forward to allow us to slowly pass through and up to the front. What a feeling of wonder and joy to be in a car in the middle of the herd, to be one with them. The horses glanced over casually, as if the car were just another horse moving along.

The moment took me back to my younger years as a child, a time in my mind when I was a horse, magnificent, beautiful, powerful, and free. Horses had always been there for me throughout childhood in all their glory, both figuratively and literally. Mr. Ed, Black Beauty, The Black Stallion, along with the others who taught me to ride and had provided the haven, the fertile grounds, where the dreams about horses started dancing within me. Like so many other young girls, they spoke to me in ways I cannot describe nor was even aware. They became my totem, best friend, and muse, with most of my free waking hours being a horse; galloping through the enchanted forest on long twiggy legs, my long red mane whipping through the wind, as I effortlessly jumped over any obstacles in my path, being in a state of pure grace.

Time passed and I grew older and somewhere along the way the horse dreams slowly started to fade into the dark recesses of my subconscious, like a burning flame that had almost been doused. But the embers were still burning, waiting for the perfect moment to be reignited.

This herd of horses seemed to graciously acknowledge and accept our presence. I was granted this chance of a lifetime and allowed to relive my childhood dream of being a horse, this time among the horses themselves. Their deep, dark, and lively eyes connected to mine through the lens of the camera; they seemed to be greeting me, asking me to join them. Feelings of glee coursed through my veins and in this moment I was truly empowered and liberated. I had finally returned home.

The ranch roundup lasted a couple of days, so on a whim my friend and I took the opportunity to see if we could locate some of the wild horses from the Sand Wash Basin bands that lived in the surrounding area. I had always wanted to see the Mustangs in their native habitat.

The winter up north had been harsh and snowy, and the thawing, rutted roads could be slippery and treacherous. As it turned out, the roads were clear. The barren and desolate terrain slowly unfolded with a color palette that was limited and monochromatic; primarily washed out hues of beige, gray, and sage. It seemed impossible that any life could be supported other than insects and lizards, yet the horses found a sustainable existence there.

The slow moving vehicle granted plenty of time to scan the horizon, searching for any evidence of horses. There were many manure piles left by the stallions marking their territory and it seemed strange that they would travel along a man-made road. Then I realized, it was probably their road long before the Bureau of Land Management came along.

Soon, a small band of horses made their presence known as they approached their watering hole very close to the road. Pulling over, excited at being a witness to such amazing beauty, I quickly fumbled for my camera as they watched with cautious curiosity. Not alarmed, it was obvious they were accustomed to vehicles passing through their land. Their eyes were riveted to mine and their gaze was intense; dark, yet luminous. Who was the spectator here? Was it them or me? Outnumbered, I could feel them looking directly into my soul.

The white stallion proudly wore the marks of many battles, which won him the right to his small harem. There was one dark foal at its mother's side, a brown and white splashy paint with a large white blaze running down his face, and a few others. Horses with unusual coloration have always intrigued me. Perhaps I relate to how they stand out in a group since my hair is red, my skin light and freckled. What makes me unique now, made me feel extremely uncomfortable as a young child. I became aware that I felt a sense of separation, singled out, different once again.

Slowly walking toward them, they moved away at about the same speed, occasionally stopping to face me and look with as much curiosity as I had for them. My human awkwardness soon went away; they were such an amazing natural sight to behold; divine in their perfection, freedom, and unity!

The late afternoon sun was shining and the mountains behind the horses made an amazing backdrop. Their home could have been heaven, and the desolation seemed to have disappeared. This is where they belonged, now and forever.

What was it that they were trying to communicate? There seemed to be an innate ancient wisdom in their eyes, a wisdom inherited from generations of their ancestors; one that humankind could learn and grow from. What I experienced was expansive, infinite, and timeless, as I sensed their presence in my heart.

I didn't stay too long, for they vanished into the landscape as quickly as they had appeared, sweeping my soul with them. The longing to join them and be a horse once again was intense; to be carefree and wild, experiencing life as it is meant to be. I too felt as though I would be absorbed into their land.

Returning to the vehicle, I felt honored and joyful, with a sense of reverence, that they had made themselves known and accessible while allowing me a sweet but short time span to witness them in all their glory and freedom. A foreign energy vibrated through my body. Feeling ecstatic, I sensed that the horses had shared their energy with me. The physical distance separating the band and me had dissipated, creating a unity between us. The heart and soul of the horses had connected intimately with the heart and soul of this human. The shadows lurking in the chambers of an aching heart immediately dispersed and in this sacred space the intimate dance of life began and my heart opened up, filling with hope and joy.

I now know that this was to prepare me for the future; for sights I was destined to see and experience. Only since connecting with the roundup horses and the wild Mustangs had I become aware, feeling in the core of my being, the polarity of the lives of the horses from the two events of that weekend: there was the display of energy and vitality of the domestic herd from the roundup juxtaposed with the freedom and unity of the wild band. They were separated by only ten or fifteen miles as a crow flies, yet a universe away in significance.

Horses had come and gone throughout my life. The horses never really left me; it was I who abandoned them. Using my photography skills soullessly in a seemingly lucrative career in marketing kept me globe-trotting, coming home exhausted and collapsing only to recover in time to start over again. Like the movie *Groundhog Day*, I was trapped in an endless loop of misery. Somewhere along the way I was bucked off my Windhorse, crashing to the ground without noticing.

Seeking spiritual advice, one healer gravely told me I had lost my life force energy. He gave me a list of what seemed like endless, tiring tasks to reclaim it. Another, an Ayurvedic practitioner, told me I was just like the charred crust on a blackened pot and she had an herbal remedy that seemed more practical to follow. Anything, I thought, to nurture myself back. I felt the depths of separation as though I were hanging by a thread to what little energy and ties to humanity I had left.

Meanwhile, the horses had lingered patiently in that darkness, waiting to be unleashed with all their creative, unbridled energy. They were on call, ready to assist me. I could leap onto their backs, to take off on my pilgrimage of reawakening and wholeness, harnessing their strength while infusing their energy.

Truth be told, it was time to allow, but even more than that, time to trust myself and give myself permission to be guided back on my life's journey; reclaiming my creative birthright by rekindling the ash-shrouded, softly-glowing embers of my passion for the horses.

Leaving the fancy jet-setting marketing career behind took courage, but the horses long corralled and buried in the past were anxious to emerge and share their messages. The images that evolved in the Windhorse series had been hidden in my memory and were now appearing as guides; courage, destiny, spirit, and others. What unfolded in the upcoming months was a sequence of events where my Windhorse would fly down from above, grab me, toss me onto her back, and I would return to my path of the horse with such intensity I would be spinning.

The artwork that evolved was laying a solid foundation for the powerful and rich excavation of my soul that was yet to come. And while I naively thought I was done healing, this was just the beginning. If there was one thing I was sure about, it was that I wanted to create and share with the world beautiful works of art embodying the voices of the horses that would elevate people's levels of consciousness; the gift the horses had given to me.

To fully reflect this in my creations, I had to be in union with my true self and listen to my heart, which connected intimately with the horses. In this connection there is an awareness of the timeless essence of the universe within and without, while simultaneously networked to all other beings like a gossamer web. Sharing this with the world through my creations was extremely important to me, and I hoped that the Windhorses would help others find the infinite silence within themselves in order to heal. My burning desire was to help both horses and people with my artwork. But I was still lacking much needed clarity.

Feeling as though I had been summoned as the horses' messenger, if I had not been called to witness them in the wild, I probably would not have gone down to participate in the Mustang adoption event I was eagerly driving toward a few weeks later. I naively thought I would be witnessing proud American Mustangs anxiously awaiting their new and loving homes. I expected crowds of people eagerly looking at the animals, anticipating and hoping to bring one home. If I had been remotely aware of what I was going to see, and the raw emotions I would feel, then perhaps I wouldn't have gone to the adoption, but run the other way. In so many ways, it was better that I didn't know.

Arriving at the fairgrounds, I could smell the familiar sweet, musky aroma of horses before I saw them. Like a homing pigeon, I quickly located them. However, it became readily apparent that my expectations were not valid. Very few people attended and by the end of the day only two Mustangs had found new homes.

Instead of finding horses contentedly munching on hay, they were tightly huddled together and cowering in misery. I saw the expressionless, glazed eyes of dissociation and the sullen body language of emotionally shut down horses. Disappointment quickly sank in. Heads were hanging limply from gaunt bodies. Their manes were knotted, fur lusterless, and their lack of muscle tone told stories of their duration in captivity. There was also the other extreme – wild and white-rimmed eyes with nostrils flaring, close to panicking as they forced their bodies against the fence, jockeying for prime positions behind one another as far away from human contact as possible. I could feel their hearts pounding. They were frightened, and rightfully so. Reduced to a marginal existence, many of these young horses seemed to display the mind-numbing symptoms of trauma victims.

Of the numerous horses contained there, I was drawn to some corrals with younger horses. Their silent voices told the same sad story of misguided and traumatic handling. It was too much for their young minds, bodies, and souls to bear. The youngest ones, probably yearlings, had their spirit sucked right out of their bodies, while some of the others corralled next to them were fighting to retain what they had left; the lucky ones still had a dim flicker of curiosity in them.

The yearlings, with their hauntingly blank eyes, stood dejectedly against the far rail, lips pursed, bodies flaccid, with numbered tags hanging off their necks like an inmate. Reduced to a numbering system, little Number 2000 had a sunny color and a sharply contrasting dark mane. The scene was reminiscent of the photos you see when they book a prisoner and take mug shots, only these little souls would not look to face my camera no matter how much I tried to encourage and coax them.

I felt a wave of sadness rush through my body as my throat and heart became constricted. I wanted to hunch over into a small ball and disappear into the dark void with them. "Go away, leave me alone," they seemed to say. Their voices continued... "What did I do wrong to get here? When am I going home? Where is my mother? I lost her when the big thing like a bird chased me into captivity. I saw my sister fall and be trampled by my terrified family. I am worried about her... Why isn't she here with the rest of us? Why is this happening to me? Set me free!" Alone, disconnected, and fragile, they only wanted themselves for comfort.

My eyes slowly traced the freeze brand on their necks. Uneducated about how to read it, I tried to make sense of the lines, which may as well have been hieroglyphics. It seemed to contain an untold nightmare about what these youngsters had experienced. Freeze branding is supposedly painless. However, for a light-colored youngster like Number 2000, the process is longer. The torturous thirteen seconds, while an iron that has been cooled to -100 to -300 degrees is applied with 35 to 45 pounds of pressure to the skin, must have felt like an eternity. I could feel the waves of nausea as they spread out from my stomach while memories of my own vulnerability flooded me. The poor little soul.

I slowly lifted the camera and focused the lens on the youngsters, questioning why I was even taking the shot. The atmosphere felt shrouded with oppression and the camera felt heavy as I waited for them to make eye contact. It seemed like eons and it didn't happen. They never looked my way or gave any indication that they knew I was there. Returning to the present, I had been transfixed and immobilized for what seemed like centuries. Taking only one shot, I retreated and slowly walked away.

In the neighboring corral I noticed two small bays, perhaps two year-olds and related, with long forelocks and wildly unkempt manes. They had the luxury of having more time on the open range witnessing more of the sweetness of roaming free with their band. Their eyes told a much different story. Wide open with the whites showing and almost rolled back up into their heads, they anticipated with fear and dread the next awaited event in their short lives. Pieces of hide were missing from their noble heads, leaving raw, exposed flesh and telling more of a story than I could bear to hear. They still had an aliveness and curiosity that told me the spirit in them had not given up, but they were clinging by a thread so as not to lose it.

Feelings of frustration, helplessness, abandonment, and sadness… "Are they mine or are they the horses'?" Perhaps both, I assume. There was a thick blanket of oppression; the end product of experiencing somebody's will forced upon you. I knew it well. So displaced and disconnected, how could anybody ever convince these creatures that somebody was doing this for their own good? One could only hope that they would soon be adopted into compassionate homes where somebody had the patience to nurse their wounded souls back to health.

Sensing they were curious about my camera, but also afraid, I took only three photos. Their skin twitched as the shutter was released. While the day was beautiful and sunny, it was laced with the darkness of their helplessness and hopelessness. What had started out as a colorful and warm spring day had rapidly turned cold and somber; black-and-white peppered with shades of gray.

It only required a total of four shots that day to feel and embody the tragedy of their story, and I soon vanished from their lives as quickly as I had appeared. My mind was furiously trying to process everything I had witnessed. I roamed the fairgrounds and visited with several local horses who call this place home. Shortly afterward, I went into the indoor arena where a local youth group was presenting a mounted performance prior to the official adoption process. It was easy in that moment for me to forget the abandoned and tormented that were waiting outside in their prisons. But, forgetting was the easy way out.

How long could their voices be buried, hiding inside me before they resurfaced? It was only a couple of weeks before the revelation happened. It was late in the evening when I finally took a close hard look at the photographs of the young Mustangs. It is always in the quiet, seductive darkness of the late evenings, working solely from intuition, when the images call and beg for resurrection.

The image of the yearlings called the loudest. "Help!" was the voice I heard when I looked at it. It resonated so strongly in the core of my being. Immediately, tears of sadness welled in my eyes. They longed and mourned for their freedom, as I did for myself, freedom from injustice, enormous loss, and a marginalized existence.

While I have witnessed the effect my art has upon others, never have I been so incredibly moved or heard their voices so clearly myself. I had been on auto-pilot most of my life. Was this a plea to help them, help myself, or help all sentient beings? Representing lost liberty and lost dreams, once again our worlds collided.

It was that night that a new Mustang series called After the Gathering was born. Sitting there, enveloped by darkness and alone, deep in the flow of creativity, I came to realize that I was no longer using the horses only as metaphors for recognizing and releasing my own trapped feelings, but also to come to their aid. I had come full circle. I had been led on a winding, slow at times, life path. Often off course and blindly crashing through uncharted territory, where I finally landed was no surprise. It was as if I had been struck by a lightning bolt, sent from a collective consciousness of ancient wisdom from all the horses that are and ever were. Indeed it is difficult to put into words, but at best can be described as a high-frequency vibrational energy that felt like, if not modulated, I would explode into millions of tiny pieces.

In that moment I knew and understood a powerful truth that there was a unity with all that exists and ever did exist, bringing with it a sense of joy and wholeness. The electrical charge of the moment flowed into and filled my soul and energized my weary spirit. Effervescently bubbling up out of the darkness, it was powerful and jolting, yet a peaceful knowingness emanated. While my heart pounded, there was also serenity as euphoria set in.

I don't think I slept at all that night. The extraordinary had taken place and inside of me dwelled the entire universe. While the universe danced in me, I was also in it. This was the moment that we all crave and desire so intensely – to know in our being that everything is perfect and *is,* and that all that we seek is already present when we open our hearts and minds to receiving it.

Now able to communicate and express the horses' voices, coupled with mine, I felt ready to represent their messages to the world. My work became charged with energy; that of hope and hopelessness, mystery and reality, sadness and joy, lightness and darkness, and clarity and confusion.

It was time to find a way to honor and give back to the horses what they had so graciously given to me. The horses had given a gift of a renewed sense of wholeness; abundance, faith, and optimism were growing inside me. Along with that came freedom from limitations, but most importantly a rejuvenation and reclamation of the vital life force energy and joy that is our birthright.

With my newly found trust, hope, and fearlessness to follow my path, while trusting the timing, it became my desire to hear their voices, share their messages, and support the numerous organizations that are in alignment with similar missions. It can only be described as a sense of knowingness, peace, and the knowledge that the universe will provide support for me along the way. I decided there is no time like the present to be an advocate for the preservation of both the wild Mustangs and the evolution of humanity.

Photography is often used to document tragedy with the hopes it will bring positive change into the world while sharing and raising the consciousness of our planet so that all beings may live in peace, love, and harmony. This became my mission.

That night I vowed that I would use the images to educate and bring awareness to people about the fight to save the last of America's wild horses. It is from this desire that I myself became more aware and currently support efforts of the organizations that have committed themselves to providing sanctuaries where the horses will roam free to peacefully live out the remainder of their lives in unity and harmony. That night I knew in my heart that I was aligned and on my path, and while it wasn't entirely clear yet, I needed to trust the journey, knowing it must be followed for it was leading me to an authentic life; a life where I honor the voices inside and live freely and fearlessly, embracing the uncharted terrain with all the horses at my side.

My life has changed forever since the sequence of events from the spring; the roundup, the Mustangs in the wild, and the Mustangs at the adoption day had all spoken to my soul in profoundly different ways, yet all inter-related. To live a life of trust and truth required that I continue to hear the voices of the horses and remain faithful on my journey as an artist and photographer. Powerful and liberating, it has become my calling, requiring me to face all my fears of the unknown, venturing forward to be of service to the horses.

The horses are calling... Listen quietly and you can hear what they are saying, for I am only their messenger.

Photo by Susan Williams

After the Gathering: XXX4

I would like to give heartfelt thanks to my life partner, Brad, who has provided me with the love, strength, and support to make this journey.

51

About
Susan Williams

Recognized nationally and internationally as a digital camera expert, Susan's evocative equine fine art photography portrays the magical and powerful essence, along with the intimate moments, of horses. Specializing in unique and distinctive contemporary equine  fine art, she is an artist who uses photography, with a painterly style, as her medium of expression.

Always passionate about horses and also an avid artist, she was invited to study fine art photography with a small group of students from around the world at the International Center for Photography in New York City, leaving her career in the sciences behind forever. Studies at ICP encouraged her to take her photography beyond visual documentation and objectification into the realm of the invisible, inviting and encouraging contemplation and participation from her audience. After attending ICP she developed and taught programs while managing a digital camera product line for Olympus America.

She has been profoundly influenced by the writing and photography of Minor White and also John Daido Loori Roshi, a student of White's. When she first read Minor's work she felt like she had come home, a place deep inside of her that could not articulate how she felt about what she was doing.

White wrote, "No matter how slow the film, Spirit always stands still long enough for the photographer It has chosen."

Other creative influences on her were photographers Keith Carter and Michael Kenna, whose work, with its ethereal nature, so eloquently captures the mystery in the everyday. She has studied with many of the great names in photography: Duane Michaels, George Tice, John Daido Loori Roshi, to name a few. Additionally, she was a teaching assistant for well known photographer Dan Burkholder.

Working with subdued color palettes enshrouds the horses with mystery, drama, and sensuality. Luminous and charged with energy, elements of mystery and the unknown are accentuated. There is never a preconceived idea for an image and she loves that the final image is a product of nothing more than an intuitive process. Many of her horses exist in a space that hovers between the familiar and the unfamiliar, allowing the imagination to soar freely. Her audience is drawn deeply into the domain of the horse where active participation is encouraged. It becomes a dance, with the horse's acting as mirrors into unseen worlds.

"Susan's equine images dance between the plains of consciousness evoking strong emotions that are sometimes uncomfortable because we feel them in our heart or core being. The ethereal use of light and shadow create both an air of mystery and of hope. Reality and dreamtime often merge, as the observer can be drawn into an image by a horse's penetrating eyes, eyes that seem to know your innermost stories, but also have their own story to tell, if you listen."

~ L. Winston, Founder of Peak Exposure

Susan's work has been exhibited around the country and also published. Collectors across the country seek her award-winning images of horses to grace their homes and businesses.

The horse is one of the most pampered creatures on this planet, along with one of the most misunderstood and abused. It has become one of Susan's missions in life to give back to organizations that support the preservation of the wild Mustangs and also domestic horses who no longer have value to their owners.

Born in England and raised in eastern United States, she found home in the mountains of Morrison, Colorado with her partner Brad and their two Friesian paint cross colts Kairos and Zephyr. They are her Windhorses and her muses. WindhorseOne Studios was born into creation when she realized how the horses had freed her soul.

Susan invites you to visit her website at www.windhorseone.com, where you may share her vision or follow her blog about a day in the life of an equine artist (www.windhorseone.blogspot.com).

Sundance: The Gift of Grace

By Stormy May

"Either exist as you are or be as you look."
~ Mevlana Celaleddin Rumi

A snort like crackling fire, a plume of a tail high above her back, the bright filly stood out from the other weanlings. She leapt like a dancer, her hooves disdaining the earth, her body hovering as she soared from one half of the round pen to the other.

Even though she was of Dutch Warmblood breeding, her Spanish name, La Mancha, spoke of the crazy dream that I was embarking on. Visions of Cervantes' Don Quixote fighting windmill-giants in his outlandish fantasies seemed an appropriate metaphor for my quest to compete in the Olympics in the sport of dressage. It was the latest goal I had set for myself after several years of college and life experience revealed that sandwiching my name between Dr. and DVM wasn't worth the stress of school. I wanted to ride horses! So, with some inherited money and a new job as a trainer at a horse-breeding farm, I purchased my young dream horse.

Glossy magazine photos fed my desire. Dressage horses were captured frozen in time, prancing with sweat glistening, braided manes, necks tightly held in just the right position, in the midst of flawlessly executing feats of athletic prowess. I read about the riders who had made it to the top with their determination and grit. I cataloged articles and collected shelves full of books further elucidating the lofty goals of dressage. I had the time, the talent, the right trainers, and now the right horse to take me all the way to the highest levels of the sport.

Even though she was only nine months old, I was eager to start her preparation. To begin La Mancha's in hand training, I haltered and led her proudly around the long circular driveway, away from the other horses. She was big for her age, but still pony-sized so I could hold on as she leapt from side to side, like a marlin caught on a fishing line, but instead of being caught with a hook, she was "caught" by a halter buckled around her head and attached to a thick cotton rope with my gripping hands at the end.

I felt her fear of being separated from the others and continued to walk on, tightly holding onto the rope and my emotions. Past experience told me that once she figured out how long the rope was, she would settle down and see that I would keep her safe from the dangers she imagined. I noted her high-spiritedness, persuading myself that it would translate into that extra "something" that would get us high scores.

The farm we lived at by the time La Mancha turned three was the perfect place to initiate her into the subtleties of mounted work. Each day for weeks before her formal training began, I would enter her corral to pick up the previous day's manure. She quickly learned that if she backed up to me, I would scratch her favorite spot, the top of her tailbone, gradually working my fingers all the way down to the bottommost tip of her spine. If she continued backing up, I scratched her more vigorously. Often I would end up backed right into the pipe panel fence. I climbed the fence and continued, moving my fingernails up her back to her withers.

One day, looking down on her sloping red back below me as I sat scratching her from the top of the fence, I felt a temptation I couldn't resist. I slipped my leg over and then was on, feeling her warm muscles through the denim of my jeans. The moment I let go of the fence and put my body completely on her back felt like symbolically letting go of control of my own life and destiny, and entrusting those moments to the mind and power of a three-year-old filly. She cocked her head to look back at my leg as it descended her side and then continued to stand as if nothing had changed. I stayed on for a moment, rubbing her withers and then slid down to the ground, thanking her for the opportunity she had given me.

I made more of that first "ride" of ours than she did. As I wheeled out the muck cart, she followed me to the gate, maybe hoping for more scratching or treats, or perhaps with some other message I couldn't understand. My mind was racing. How effortless it had been; surely that was the start of a great mounted partnership. She was so easy to get on, not seeming to mind me on her back one bit. Once again I fantasized about the competitions we'd win, the places we'd travel to, and the adoration we'd gain.

After a few more mounted scratching sessions, I figured it was time for "serious" training. For that, I got a large loose ring snaffle bit and an oversized bridle and started getting her accustomed to having a piece of metal in her mouth and a small leather pad on her back with a strap tightened behind her forelegs.

I taught her to run around in circles, attached to me by a long cotton line, otherwise known as the discipline of longeing. That was when I started to realize just what she was capable of. A panicked horse usually does one of two things; she either freezes, or tries to flee. La Mancha chose the latter, turning into a huge red mass of bone, hoof, and muscle leaping so high that she brushed tree branches with her hind legs. The fact that I was attached to that 1200-pound phenomenon by a line running through my thinly gloved hands shook my confidence. The hundreds of years of Warmblood breeding that culminated in this powerfully athletic chestnut mare presented me with something I could barely understand or control.

In my imagination, when I placed myself on top of her, what resulted could be classified as mentally-induced terror. The thought of what might happen to my body if she ever performed those sorts of leaps with me aboard was the beginning of an underlying doubt that, as self-confident as I seemed, made me question how to proceed.

I gingerly started mounting her with bated breath, no longer free in the corral, but as a rider mounting a horse, fully appointed with saddle, bridle, bit, whip, helmet, and protective vest. Was I riding into battle on my chestnut steed, or to battle *with* my chestnut steed?

Typically she seemed to tolerate my presence on her back for several minutes, until something changed and her feet left the ground in a leap, buck, or bolt. I became skilled at twisting in the air as I looked for the best landing spot, trying to ensure that I landed on my backside rather than my front side.

Her next tactic, when I got back on, as I always did, was to plant her feet and not move. I would sit in the saddle, looking out through a cloud of fear disguised as an attitude of "you'd better do this *or else*" with my legs, seat, and whip mechanically commanding her to go, while the rest of my petrified being prayed feverishly for her to stay put.

Motivated by fear, I began to seek out "experts" to advise me on how to deal with a horse of this caliber. I thought she needed a rider who was relaxed and confident in the saddle. And I wasn't that rider. While teaching at a riding camp, I described my problem to another one of my colleagues, one whose former careers included the rough world of conditioning racehorses and Three Day Eventers. This six-foot Amazon woman seemed like the type who had real confidence and wouldn't take "no" or even "maybe" for an answer. It was threatening to my self-image that another trainer might be able to do what I couldn't, but I hoped that she had a special trick that would make La Mancha relax and settle into her role so that I could get on with the business of readying her for competition.

When I called to check on her, I received reports of how well my horse was doing out on the trails, walking through creeks, up hills, and with other horses. I believed what I heard, but something cynical inside of me warned, "Yeah, but that woman's different. She'll still misbehave for me."

When it was time to pick her up, we scheduled enough time for me to ride her in the arena. From the moment I stood next to La Mancha, ready to mount, I felt the old familiar fear creeping back in.

"Sit up, shorten your stirrups, relax your arms, hold this whip," the trainer directed as she placed in my hand a thick jockey's whip with leather strips poking out like ruffled feathers on a turkey's neck. The queasy, insecure feeling intensified and I had the thought, "What good is this horse if she doesn't do what I want?" In essence, I was really asking, "What good is this horse if I feel scared on her back?" After holding back tears and willing myself to do as the trainer said, I dismounted, thanked her, and assured her that I would let her know how it went in the coming weeks. After a few rides on La Mancha at home, my fears were confirmed. Nothing had changed.

I continued to go through the motions of training, figuring that this was the grit and determination the top riders were referring to. There would be days when she graced me with a trot that was far beyond anything I had experienced on horseback, or a canter that was so balanced that I felt I could hang in the air on that gentle rocking chair stride forever, the feeling of heaven descended to earth. But those moments were rare and the other moments built themselves into a nightmarish sequence of tension, pulling, kicking, whipping, and the occasional flight of my body through the air and the inevitable thud on the ground.

I was still convinced that the methods I had learned from my own instructors would eventually be a language that La Mancha understood. It seemed logical that I needed to start with as much force as necessary to get the correct response and then over the course of months and years, I'd be able to refine the cues down to the softest, often imperceptible shifts of weight and energy. This was the way that horses had been trained for hundreds of years, resulting in what I pictured as a horse lightly performing ballet with a rider sitting motionless in perfect mental and physical communion.

Eventually our rides became predictable. We would begin with a 15 to 30 minute fight about going forward, and then it felt as if a switch would flip and La Mancha would float forward into any gait I chose from only a hint of a cue. It felt like I was being teased; the ecstatic feeling of what she was capable of hung elusively out of my control, subject to something I searched desperately to understand. I was so relieved by the time she went forward that I would ride for about five minutes longer and then dismount, hoping that the next day she would remember those last minutes positively and start out where we left off. That was never to be the case.

What was wrong? After vet visits ruled out physical problems and the more extreme methods of forcing her didn't work, I went searching for something different. I read books on natural horsemanship and horse whispering. Most of these were essentially the same techniques I'd studied for years in new packages, with florid terminology and clever exercises mixed in. When they failed to work, I looked for something gentler. I saddled her up and sat on her for hours at a time, without giving even one squeeze, waiting for it to be her idea to move off at a brisk walk or hopefully a nice controlled trot. We sat as still as knights on a forgotten chessboard.

In the meantime, my training business was burgeoning and I was ready to start my own horse ranch. I found an affordable 9-acre parcel of land in the Sierra Nevada foothills of Northern California and moved up with my little herd. Soon, a changing menagerie of other horses in for training or rehabilitation filled the corrals.

My new start was when I decided that I also needed a new start with La Mancha. I thought it would help if I changed her name to something that brought up fewer images of futile, insane fights against false giants with big whirling arms, and more images of dancing, lightness, and artistic ventures. *Sundance*. The name conjured up images of Robert Redford and his edgy film festival bringing innovation to the film world, as well as dancing, a metaphor that I aspired to in my relations with horses, and of course the sun, that unimaginably big mass of energy that shines on everyone equally and makes life on this planet possible.

New name and all, Sundance's days at the ranch continued in the same pattern that had been established at other farms we had lived at. My business partner thought I should get rid of her. He reasoned that she was eating a lot of hay and generating piles of manure and nothing that he or I had done had brought her any closer to being the riding horse I dreamed of. Eleven years had passed since I first put my leg over her back, and the guilt, regret, and hopelessness I felt competed with the sense of responsibility for her life I took on when I bought her. Even if I wanted to find her another home, who would take an athletic Warmblood mare who clearly expressed what she thought of training?

I spoke to a fellow instructor who seemed eager when she saw pictures of the well-built purebred mare. She told me she'd like to breed her to her Appaloosa stallion in her quest to develop a spotted breed of sport horses. At the beginning of breeding season I dropped her off with an assurance that if she didn't work out as a broodmare, I would take her back, alleviating some of the guilt I felt in sending her away. I took the time to return to my life as a horse trainer without that red mark in the pasture reminding me every day of my failure.

After an ultrasound revealed that she hadn't become pregnant, the woman hauled her back to my ranch. As I saw those red hindquarters emerging from the trailer, I felt the feeling of hopelessness returning, and also an unexpected feeling of relief that my mare was back.

There are times in a person's life when everything feels like it's falling apart. Late summer and early fall of 2006 were like that for me. I had created a name for myself in the United States Pony Club organization wearing the hats of instructor, Chief Horse Management Judge, and National Examiner. I traveled around the country to Pony Club rallies, ratings, meetings, and camps. At home I balanced a ranch full of horses in training and regular clients spread across Northern California. Wherever I went I would smile and say "Excellent" to anyone who asked how I was doing.

But the reality was different. On my travels, I started noticing that the kids and horses were mostly scared, resigned, or expressing a hyper-excitement, seeming to cover either a performance anxiety or fear of the horse they were with. In my own life I had become such an expert at hiding my own feelings that I simply felt a dull repetition of working horses, driving to lessons, and looking forward to a stop at a gas station for a quick pick-me-up of iced tea and chocolate.

I kept returning to Sundance with a mix of desperation and quixotic hope. While searching for solutions to my problems with her over the years, I had compiled a short list of people who I considered to be equine geniuses. Their books weren't what I would classify as natural horsemanship; they had more of a *horse conscious* focus, considering the horse as a source of wisdom and guidance in their lives. I applied their ideas with varying levels of success, but still nothing seemed to make Sundance fit into my Olympic-sized box.

The Olympic dream slowly faded and I started noticing another dream asking to be born. Seeing Sundance in the pasture called like a siren, begging me to jump into an unknown ocean with the promise of unity if I could survive the swim to the other side. The form of the dream, the Olympics, became less important than the moments I was living with my horse. I asked myself what it would take to enjoy being with her. Was it possible to find real harmony between horses and humans or was that sentiment made of the same cloth that made up the emperor's new clothes, visible only to those who are afraid of being thought a fool or poseur? Was it just a fantasy we created to justify our own human agendas? Something told me these people on my list had found deeper answers that hadn't been conveyed in their books.

I decided to make a documentary about the search to find a real partnership between horses and humans. It was a good excuse to meet the people on my list and do some detective work, not only for my own benefit, but for others who were at similar crossroads in their lives with horses.

But how was a horse trainer with no film background going to pull this one off? After looking into grants and corporate sponsors, the problem of funding was solved when I took stock of my own assets, which were tied up in the ranch I had bought three years earlier. I looked ahead 30 years and saw that I could still be teaching the same lessons, training new horses to do the same things, talking about the same topics, and paying the same mortgage. Or, I could sell the ranch and use the money to fly around the world trying to unearth a secret from people I'd only read about.

During the course of filming the documentary, the secret did start to unfold. My first trip to Russia was the point of no return. I remember the moment as my guide Georgui sat on the floor looking at a laptop computer propped on the seat of a wooden chair. Georgui was a photographer for the *Nevzorov Haute Ecole* magazine, which was published by the man I had come to interview, Alexander Nevzorov. Georgui was excited about putting his photographs together in a specific sequence so it would look like a stop-action film. He showed me how he had already started putting them in order. His excitement was incongruous with the pictures that flashed on the screen.

These pictures were taken at horse shows. The horses belonged to different breeds, were different colors with different riders representing different disciplines, but the common subject in each photograph was a human causing a horse pain. These were not the slick magazine photos that I thought were an accurate representation of horse sports. These were those same riders in other moments. The scenes were ones I recognized. The photographs showed terrified animals with stiff necks, bulging eyes, flaring nostrils, mouths wrenched open, tongues askew, and saliva streaming. I had seen some of the pictures before on Nevzorov's website so I thought I'd be prepared for more, but now I found myself sitting in a dingy Russian apartment with the photographer who had witnessed these events, busily telling me how he was going to make a short film to teach people how to capture the moment with a digital camera.

"You took all these photos?" I asked, trying to make sense of what I was seeing.

"Yes," he replied, "I go to competitions almost every weekend."

"How can you stand to watch the horses being treated like that?" I asked, wondering if he had a sadistic streak in him. I knew I was wrong when I saw sadness expose itself from underneath his chattering. His voice lowered and grew unsteady as he said, "It's really horrible. It makes me sick to see, but it must be documented, so I'll take these pictures and show the world. I know I won't be able to do it much longer so I'm going to teach others how to do it." When he finished, I felt for a moment the wounded heart of this young man, standing back and witnessing those crimes through the lens of his camera. It felt like he was a war journalist documenting human bodies in the throes of the most intense pain, but helpless to intercede in the name of objective reporting.

I knew that I was guilty of contributing to this microcosm of pain and suffering in the world. I had even directed it toward those beings I said I loved the most – the horses. I realized that the only thing gentle and horse conscious about my own methods were that they weren't quite as extreme as other people used. I could say those other riders were cruel, but we were all cut from the same cloth; we wanted to use horses to make us look and feel good about ourselves. In that moment, I knew that Georgui's cause was now mine as well. I sat beside him feeling the immensity of the task ahead. After a timeless moment he closed the computer and started talking about where we were going to eat.

A few days after returning from Russia, my internal clock was still half a world away as I went out before sunrise to feed the horses. After finishing, I noticed a full-grown robin standing on the ground near the bales of hay. There was something un-birdlike about how he was standing, so still with ruffled feathers and blinking eyes. I gently folded my legs and sat on the ground about six feet in front of him. He seemed content to simply stand and rest and watch me a little. After what felt like 10 minutes he started walking toward me, then he circled away and then back toward me. He was a little unsteady on his legs, but otherwise, I could find no explanation for his behavior. We sat about two feet apart for another period of time and then he walked closer until he was six inches from my left knee. He turned and we sat side by side, like friends looking out at the scenery.

I wanted to hold him in my hand, but in that small desire I perceived the seed of forcing myself on another being. I chose to do things differently. Instead of what I wanted, I asked myself what he needed, what could I do for this bird? I made myself just sit and be with him, to become as quiet as possible inside myself. The thought of him sitting in my hand kept returning, so eventually I wondered if we shared the same sentiment. Instead of reaching out toward him and picking him up, I put my empty hand out flat in front of me and after several minutes he walked around from my left side and stepped into my hand... and then closed his eyes. We stayed that way for quite some time. I cupped him in my hands and he was very still. Over an hour passed, and my legs began to cramp, so I put my hand back down, wondering if he'd like to go. He stayed still, although I could see his balance wasn't good. I tenderly carried him with me to a nearby chair where we could sit and catch the first rays of sun. Another few minutes passed and I noticed him beginning to twitch. He was getting ready to die. I held him comfortably as he went through the death process, then buried him at the foot of a nearby tree.

Soon after, I called my students together. I showed a videotape of one of Alexander's students and told them that I wouldn't be teaching the same lessons anymore. I offered to continue coaching if anybody wanted to stop riding and start working horses without restriction or force. The uncomfortable silence in the room confirmed my suspicion that this step was too far for most people to even understand. At that point it didn't matter; it was my path. The peaceful feeling of being there with the robin confirmed what could happen if I let go of my personal agendas.

A new clarity told me that this is where Sundance had been trying to guide me all along. Grace had knocked at my door in the form of a fiery filly. After failing enough times, I began to understand that the control I desperately sought moment by moment had become my addiction. I saw human life as it truly is, not a safe movie with a predictable ending, but a constant yet fragile movement toward some things and away from others. By seeing and accepting Sundance's authentic expression, I was able to uncover what was happening inside myself, seeing beyond the struggles of trying to be safe in the world. She had consistently shown me exactly what I needed to know in order to be with her. In truth, I had been the student, she my teacher all along.

⁎

I moved my home into a spiritual community as I was putting the final touches on the documentary a month before its release. My herd moved to a large meadow situated in the center of the community's houses. I settled into a new life without the pressure of lessons or horses in training, and with enough money in the bank to wait out the period needed to determine if the film would be profitable.

I walked in the pasture several months after the completion and release of the documentary with its accompanying flurry of sales and complimentary reviews. It was a beautiful late fall day with the sun slanting down, nearly touching the treetops, illuminating the coats of the grazing horses. I felt leaves still crunchy under my feet where a light rain had not penetrated. The smell of wet bark and moist earth entered my nose like gentle, smokeless incense enveloping my thoughts.

I took one step toward Sundance and paused as her head turned almost imperceptibly away and her eyelids flickered and tensed. I stood still for a moment, and then stepped back. As I did, Sundance's head turned toward me, and her eyes relaxed. As I stepped further away, she let out a strong snort into the prickly brown grasses surrounding her nose. Still backing away, I softly walked an arc toward her hindquarters and she turned as a dancer following the cue to face her partner. I took one more step back and she picked up her nose. With a soft eye and pricked ears, she closed the distance between us, lifting her head high above mine, exposing her chest for me to scratch. As my fingernails found the old familiar grooves, she stretched her neck and leaned into my hands. This was our dance of grace in the last rays of sun, the stadium a grassy meadow, our spectators a pair of twittering bluebirds.

Sundance

I would like to thank and acknowledge those people who have watched the Path of the Horse documentary and then have been inspired to take on the challenge of seeing and doing things differently. Whether it's one person or a community living from a more authentic space, we can feel and connect to a greater force that can change our lives and the lives of those around us.

✳

About
Stormy May

After spending over 20 years as part of the traditional horse world, Stormy started looking for different ways of understanding horses. Her search led her around the world as she studied and interviewed people who each held a piece of this larger vision.

The Path of the Horse DVD documents this search. This provocative film has shaken up the horse world, sparking discussions, asking the viewer to take an honest look at current practices within the equine industry and to decide for him or herself what the next step is. Stormy's current projects include exploring the human-animal connection with her horses Patrik, Sundance, and Sofi, and writing articles as well as a full-length book investigating this topic.

For more information about Stormy and *The Path of the Horse* DVD, visit www.stormymay.com.

Through the Eyes of a Horse

By Mary Beth Meyers

Spring had arrived and I found myself loading the truck and trailer with the usual equipment and feed necessary for a dressage show. This show was located in my home territory, and I was looking forward to spending time with family and friends. It was also the first show that Antares and I would test our partnership. The anticipation made the process of preparing for the weeklong trip flow effortlessly.

My goal was to continue my education in dressage to the highest level of Fédération Equestre Internationale (FEI), the governing body for Olympic equestrian disciplines, and eventually become a judge. Having spent years of training and competing successfully at the six standard levels, I had needed a new equine partner to fulfill my dream of competing at the four international levels, up to Grand Prix. The training and preparation to reach the highest levels would be rigorous and demanding. I needed a horse who was generous and willing, and who would enjoy the challenges of such intricate work.

Loading the bales of hay lying next to the truck would be my last chore for the day. The sun had warmed the bales and I couldn't resist consciously taking in a deep breath to absorb the fragrance of the freshly cut hay. Reaching down to a bale, I pulled out several pieces of hay and placed one of the pieces in my mouth. A feeling of contentment permeated my body as I sat down quietly to re-check my list, then I hoisted the bales onto the bed of the truck and drove home to get ready for an early morning departure to the show.

The next day, as I walked toward my barn at dawn, with the early morning dew hanging heavily from the evergreen trees' spring growth, I felt reassured after listening to the weather report that the fog would be burned off by late morning. "Great!" I thought to myself. "The day should be perfect."

69

Eagerly grasping the wet handles of the heavy barn door, I slid it across the gravel, revealing the horses, who were eagerly awaiting their morning breakfast. Anxiety, tinged with excitement, brought back memories of my first show, lying awake till late the night before, captive to my young imagination envisioning what the thrill of the next day would be like. I had visions of clearing every jump without knocking down a rail, and the anticipated fun of playing games on horseback at the end of the day.

Antares' intense stare brought me back to the present, his large brown eyes vividly displaying his anticipation of breakfast and carrots. Familiar with the morning routine, he stretched his long, elegant neck over the stall opening and gently nuzzled my arm. Looking into his radiant eyes caused me to recall our first meeting.

Antares had swept me off my feet by his deep, liver-chestnut color and white socks that seemed to be painted like a piece of fine art. He stood strikingly tall at 17.2 hands high, and exuded the confidence of a warrior. It was much more than his physical beauty that drew me to him. How could one not see the inner wisdom and generosity that reflected from deep within his eyes? Antares' expression of inner strength spoke directly to my heart.

As Antares stood contentedly foraging through his hay, I ran my hands carefully down his legs. Ensuring that he had not injured himself during the night, I gathered the shipping wraps from the trunk in front of his stall. Securing the last wrap, I gave Antares' glistening coat a quick brush. We headed toward the trailer, my excitement increasing with each step as the reality of my dream closed in.

Refreshed from having spent two nights with family and friends, I was introspective during the morning drive to the show grounds. The view of the Snake River and the surrounding hills transported me back to endless days of my adolescence spent with friends galloping freely on the beach. Clad only in swimming attire, we would jump our horses off the end of the dune and then race to the middle of the river and back. Once we were back on the beach, the horses would shake wildly to remove the excess water and we would laugh while trying to stay on their bare backs.

My time of arrival at the show grounds was perfect. My students and I had decided to arrive a day early so our horses could rest. We shared much joy and laughter as we arranged to meet the next day before the competition to exercise our horses and tune up our skills before the event started.

The next day, I reminded myself to check into the show office to pick up my competitor's packet and exhibitor number. As I entered the area, the parking lot came into full view; it was filled with trucks and horse trailers. The swirl of dust rising brought my attention to the warm up arena. Both hands grasped the steering wheel, my shoulders tightened, and I began to feel the rush of nerves stream through my body.

As I unloaded Antares from the trailer, he appeared to be observing the activities surrounding his stall as though he were conducting an orchestra. I was pleased that he looked content and rested. As I called out his name, he moved his head up and down – his signal that it was time to go out for his walk. Those arriving that morning were organizing the buckets, wheelbarrows, and bales of straw they had brought with them. I buckled the leather halter around Antares' head, then glanced down the aisle.

Further down the aisle stood a tall liver-chestnut, looking very much like my own horse, except for the heavy bandaging on his legs that hid any potential white markings. I could see that the owner had just brought him out of his stall. His steps were slow and guarded, but the woman leading him was distracted and didn't notice his reluctance to walk. The gelding's walk was tentative, as though he wanted to stop and stretch, but his owner missed the cue and continued to walk him. As they passed by, I observed his stiffness. I could see that walking was not resolving his apparent discomfort. I felt anxious about his well-being as they headed to the arena for his warm-up and I finished walking Antares.

Hearing the announcer call the first exhibitor to the arena, I knew that the show had begun. I looked at my watch, rechecked my scheduled ride time, and began to set out my equipment to be used for the day. I estimated that I would need an hour for braiding, and that would give me extra time to focus on my test. Each single, one-inch braid, tied and gently tightened with yarn, represented a particular part of my test that I rehearsed and memorized. As I reached into my groom box, I discovered that I had left my braiding equipment at home. I looked around for one of my students to see if they had materials I could borrow. No luck. I wondered if the vendors had opened. Conveniently, the show office was located in the same building as the vendors and show arena. Still needing to pick up my exhibitor's packet, I knew I could stop at the office on my way to the vendors.

As I stepped into the indoor arena the stillness was apparent. The only audible sound was the rider making last moment preparations. Rounding the corner near the entrance door I had just come through, the big, bright chestnut looked toward me, beckoning my attention. I caught a vague glimmer of his dark, receded eye. I was sure that this was the horse I saw being led from his stall upon my arrival at the barn. My eyes transfixed onto his; I felt I was being pulled through a timeless vortex. The once seemingly fluorescent arena light now seemed dim. The low hum of voices had faded away. Everything around me seemed to disappear into a fog. No sound, no feeling; an almost empty stage. Suddenly, the shrill sound of the whistle signaling the rider to begin her test awakened me from the recesses of my mind. The lights became very bright. I lost contact with the chestnut's eyes momentarily. Before I realized, I found myself sitting on the edge of a hard surface, obligingly watching and listening to his thoughts of being judged. Seemingly drained and void of expression, what remaining energy emanating from his mind seeped toward me. Stilled by this contact, immediate surges of empathy rushed into every cell of my body. I knew at that moment the chestnut gelding was not present in his body. I wanted to reach him through my mind and let him know I was not judging him, but wanted to help and protect him. Looking once again at his body, I couldn't help imagining how different he would be if he were in a state of mind of true health and happiness.

I looked at the rider briefly; long enough that I could see the strain and discomfort of her body. She appeared emotionally disconnected from her horse. Her body leaned backward, chin tucked tight toward her chest, and, with heels bearing spurs, she continually jabbed against the horse's ribs. The rider's eyes were flat, no joy or happiness there, at least that I could detect.

Somehow the chestnut managed to understand the rider's requests. Or had his body just memorized every movement? I wondered what he must have been feeling in his body, if anything at all. I closed my eyes to picture in my mind what kind of an experience this would be for him. It was difficult to imagine.

I opened my eyes to see that the rider was beginning the first movement of her test. As the judge stood to acknowledge the rider's salute, the chestnut gelding stood quietly, head bowed, eyes staring at the ground, appearing to be defeated before the test had even begun.

I had seen this rider before at shows and heard that her goal was to become a judge. Could she sense her horse's thoughts or actually feel his syncopated gaits? I heard whispers behind me, questions being asked. I could not answer, as I was listening carefully to the voice and thoughts of the horse. My legs would not move. A voice in my head said, "It's time to get your braiding material." I ignored the message, staying to watch the chestnut gelding.

The rider and horse were now standing immobile in front of the judge's stand. The rider paused, adjusted her reins, and asked her horse to step backward. There was no response from the chestnut gelding. The rider tightened the grip on the reins and leveraged a stronger pull on his mouth. Responding to the increased tension, the chestnut curled his neck and tucked his chin, awkwardly taking a few steps back. Immediately, with a touch of the whip, she asked her horse to trot and make preparations for the next movement. The judge's expression was a look of displeasure as he whispered his comments and scores to the secretary.

Alarmed by the swell of emotion cascading into my body, my eyes began to fill with tears. My throat was dry and I felt a lump forming. Everything seemed to be in slow motion. The rider, anticipating the next movement, tilted her rigid body forward and used her hands to correct the position of her horse's head. I just wanted the test to be done.

As I sat there wondering why I was feeling so much emotion watching this horse and rider, I thought back to my roots growing up with a horse. How did I get from there to here? I was struck by my immediate thoughts: "Where am I on my path with horses? Am I at some level of being unconscious of horses' needs as I serve my own?" Suddenly, I saw myself in a spiral, a vortex, spinning in deep thoughts about my journey. "Why doesn't this seem right?"

Childhood memories came flooding in as tears rolled down my cheeks. My memories took me back to my father's veterinary clinic and barn, which shared the same piece of property with our house. In fact, I spent much more time at the clinic than in my family home.

My father began to teach me at a very young age how to handle and care for animals coming into the clinic for routine exams and those that had been seriously injured or traumatized. How they were injured was never my concern when they arrived at the clinic. My responsibilities were to care for and comfort the animals.

Many times I would be awakened in the middle of the night to assist in emergency calls to the clinic. The animals we cared for ranged from colicky horses to cats or dogs that had been hit by a car, to deer, skunks, and goats. I was often there to hold the animals that needed to be euthanized, a task that gave me a sense of responsibility. I felt fortunate to be able to hold them to their last breath on this earth.

The most exciting time of the year was foaling season. Helping to bring a foal into this world was exhilarating. Either I was at the back end of the mare helping to pull the foal, or I was at the front end talking to the mare, doing my best to let her know that everything would be OK. Many times I had to help carry the new-born over to the mare, particularly after a long foaling process, rubbing the colt or filly gently with a towel and clearing out their nostrils. The absolute best part was watching the foal attempt to get up for the first time, struggling to gain its first experience with gravity and then search for food. This was my first found love of being in awe of nature's great gift. I was hooked, and knew from these experiences that I would always be connected to the horses. The picture in my mind was clear. I knew from these experiences that I would not only have horses, but be a guardian of them all my life.

My thoughts came back to the arena as I saw the look of weariness on the chestnut's beautiful head as his fatigued eyes moved back and forth expecting the rider to release the reins. Sweat trickled down his legs. The shuffling of his hooves made narrow furrows in the soft, clay dirt. The rider finally softened her position and released a very loud sigh. Her white, gloved hands gave the reins forward as if to finally recognize her horse's effort.

The chestnut quickly took advantage, lengthened, and shook his head as he attempted to release the strain of being held too tight. The rider straightened her jacket, leaned forward, and gave him a gratuitous pat. She smiled at the judge and walked past the stand. Looking up momentarily, the judge nodded to her and returned to scoring the rider's test sheet.

In my view, the scores were most likely going to be based on an insufficient score for her effort. Surely, the score for the chestnut would be very high – if a score were given for his generous heart. I had no doubt he would have won the class on his own merit. Sitting silently, I closed my eyes to keep the picture of the chestnut gelding etched in my mind. I wanted him to know that his generosity had not gone unnoticed.

Feeling disturbed and agitated, I turned away from the arena to look for the vendors, and lifted my feet off the bleacher, noticing how less enthusiastic my steps were than when I had arrived at the barn this morning. As I approached the end of the barn, I caught Antares' eye, while he was quietly observing the activity of his stable mates that were being groomed and polished for the day's events. Instantly, I was reminded of the stark contrast of looking into the chestnut horse's eyes and that of my own horse. The richness and depth of color emanating from those orbs always tell the story of the horses' rich and wonderful wisdom. Their eye entices you into their world, wanting to engage and know more about you. This was in contrast to the dark, clouded eye that spoke of pain, worry, and fear, which I knew was true for the chestnut gelding.

I reached into the bag that held my newly purchased braiding tools and pulled out the soft black yarn and needle. As I lay the mane over and began braiding in the yarn, the feeling of anger and empathy were being woven into each braid. My normal routine of focusing on my test while braiding was not working this time. My mind was wandering back to the arena and that morning's experiences. Looking at my watch, I increased my pace to make up time for staying and watching the chestnut's performance. Grooming Antares' tail and wiping down the equipment would be the last thing to do before tacking him.

After pulling on my boots and taking my jacket from the bag, I grabbed my test booklet and gloves and walked next to Antares to the warm up arena. Checking my equipment one last time before mounting, I stroked his soft muzzle and gave him his favorite treat. Ears pricked forward, Antares heard the noisy wrapper and gently reached for his peppermint. Hesitant to mount, I fidgeted with the bridle and checked the girth one last time. I knew I should be starting my warm up, but I was not ready. A reluctance perhaps, or a second thought at being more aware of what I was about to ask of my horse, wanting to be sure that I was listening to Antares and knowing that the chestnut gelding would not be forgotten.

As I mounted, I looked down at the freshly woven braids in Antares' mane and tried to not think about this morning's experience. Lifting the flap on the saddle, I made one more adjustment to tighten the girth as I took note of the number of competitors warming up before entering the arena. My family and students had gathered to watch my preparation for my class. All eyes were on Antares, anxiously waiting to see him perform the higher levels of dressage. As I approached the arena, I began to recall the emotions I had experienced watching the chestnut gelding.

As I began my warm up, I could hear Antares' hooves strike the ground rhythmically and feel him take charge; he was not listening to the distracting chatter running through my mind. Flashes of the chestnut gelding's eye appeared and then disappeared, again. Sensations of the chestnut gelding's wincing stride filtered into my body. My back tightened. Stopping, I leaned forward and rounded my back in hopes of releasing the tension. Drawing in a deep breath and before returning to my warm up, I reached down and gave Antares a pat on the neck. As I asked him to perform more technical movements, I could feel my timing was off. I began to make subtle corrections and changes to the exercises, in hopes of regaining the feel of the wonderful ride from the previous day. Feeling that I was trying too hard to fix the warm up, I walked Antares over to visit with my family and students for a few minutes to relieve the stress emanating from the busy show arena – and from my mind.

I gathered up my jacket and made my preparation before entering the show arena. The exhilaration, the joy of getting to perform with such a beautiful horse seemed to be different than what I had imagined as I was driving to the show. Usually, competing came easy for me. I had overcome many unforeseen physical and mental obstacles in past shows. This was an entirely new obstacle and one that I knew I could not muscle my way through. My thoughts were winding around in my head in ways that I had not experienced before. The spark of excitement from the previous months of preparation leading up to this moment seemed dim as to what I had experienced the day before. A current of doubt threaded its way though my body as I approached the same door to enter the arena as the chestnut horse did a short time earlier. Was my heart going to be in this ride?

Antares entered the arena with his head held high looking out into the crowd. He knew he was being watched and as a result became much more animated than he was in the warm up arena. His steps had more spring and I knew his sensitivity to my cues had increased. Pleased that he was attentive and alert, I came to a halt to organize my thoughts. Sensing that he was enjoying this experience brought a smile to my face, although the undercurrent of distraction from thoughts of the chestnut gelding, intermixed with memories of my childhood and the pressure to have a flawless performance, overwhelmed me as I began my test. My nerves were interfering with my timing and I was unable to regain the fluidity of the ride from the day before. My simple goal was to maintain my focus and not allow distractions. But I felt myself pressing even to do that.

Antares continued to persevere with patience, and once again seemed to not be affected by my struggle to remain focused on the test. The movements that required transitions from one gait to the other using split second timing were tense. The performance was not fluid. The ride had not gone the way I planned; the inner conflict was insurmountable.

A feeling of disappointment surged through my body, as I knew I had let my family and students down. Our debut in the show arena was met with challenges that I had not experienced before. Powerful holograms of my experience that morning flashed repeatedly in front of me. Reeling from the pictures and quickly dismounting, I loosened Antares' girth and headed back to the barn to un-tack and cool him out after the strenuous ride.

Antares appeared to be fresh and ready to compete again, and I was happy to see him wanting to do more. My family and students continued watching the dressage show, which allowed quiet time for myself. While grooming Antares, my sense of pride began to return. Wrapping my arms around his beautiful neck, I hugged him until he lifted me off the ground. As his wisdom and heart spoke to me in a resonating voice, I recalled the chestnut gelding, who had seen a piece of my future and reflected those images vividly to me. I couldn't bear to think what I would have become had I gone crashing down the same path as the owner of the chestnut gelding.

I began to question whether I should continue to pursue my dreams of training to Grand Prix. Had I been riding to my own dream or the illusion of a dream that belonged to someone else?

The messages the chestnut gelding had given me were subtle and crept into the cracks of my image, pulling me into his world. The fire growing inside was not to pursue showing Grand Prix, but to allow the horses to guide my work. I knew in those moments that my future purpose would be restoring the health and relationships of humans and horses. What mattered most was that I continued to learn to listen to the horses.

What had been revealed to me the day of the competition opened my mind and cast new light onto my path. From that moment on my life changed. I will always maintain and guard the well-being of the horse, never allowing myself to be consumed by asking the horse to serve my needs.

The chestnut gelding brought me back into alignment with the values I learned as a child. Through the eyes of a horse, I had been asked to alter my course.

What I won the day I met the chestnut gelding was not ribbons or glory. It was the knowledge that horses have great messages for us. They speak to us often.

The question is: Are we listening?

Photo by Scarlett Pflugrad

Antares

To Tyler and Clay, who will always inspire me... my father, who never questions and is always supportive. My friend and client, Patty, who has always been steadfast. Thank you!

About
Mary Beth Meyers

With wisdom cultivated from over fifty years of working with horses, Mary Beth Meyers has created a holistic approach to building harmonious relationships between riders and their horses. Creator of Harmonic Riding – Equine Integral Movement (HREIM), Mary Beth has been a leader in the field of equine health, behavior, and bio-mechanics.

Photo by Heather Phelps

Having trained and taught children for over thirty years, an involvement in three-day eventing, dressage, (FEI) competition, thoroughbred horse racing, hunter/jumper, western showing and rodeos, and the creation of a handicap riding program, Mary Beth has had an enriching exposure to humans in action with horses.

Her passion about the health of the horse led Mary Beth onto the path of becoming a healer of relationships between horse and human. HREIM is focused on the health and welfare of the horse's spirit. It is a process grounded in decades of personal study and observation and supported by current research in the physiology of behavior.

Growing up the daughter of a veterinarian in Eastern Washington, Mary Beth was exposed to a daily life of assisting with a variety of animals at her father's clinic, which directly inspired her to create the work that she is currently doing with all animals.

Through Morven Park International Equestrian Institute, Leesburg, Virginia, Mary Beth completed a nine-month Riding Instructors Certification Program. She then moved to Southern California to pursue her passion with horses and become an assistant trainer and teacher with a Combined Training and Hunter/Jumper stable. Eventually, she returned to Washington to continue a career with horses and become a free lance instructor and trainer working with children and adults.

Mary Beth operates her training facility in Snohomish, Washington. She is an advanced student of Ramtha's School of Enlightenment, and travels throughout the United States giving HREIM workshops and providing her healing work to all animals and people.

For more information about Mary Beth and her programs, visit www.harmonicriding.com

Another Chance

By Anna Twinney

In over a decade of teaching horsemanship, I have learned that the most important lessons people get from my clinics often have nothing to do with technique, method, or even horsemanship. I've also found that the lessons we want to learn, in many cases, aren't the ones we need the most. The life-changing lessons come when we aren't looking and when we least expect them.

Some may read the stories I've written and think they are sad or tragic, and only about the grim subject of death. But, if you look closer, you will discover so much more.

The tales that follow are about rebirth, second chances, and the possibility of not only surviving tragedy, but learning, growing, and becoming better for the experience. No one asks for misfortune or heartache to walk through their door, but when it does we have the choice to shrink and hope we survive mostly intact, or stand and face it, allowing it to strengthen our hearts and make us wiser in the process.

The famous psychiatrist, Dr. Elisabeth Kübler-Ross once said, "Should you shield the canyons from the windstorms, you would never see the beauty of their carvings."

For me these stories are examples of the depth of the lessons the horses have to teach us, if we are only willing to open our hearts and listen. I hope these canyon carvings speak to your heart as deeply as they did to mine.

The Return of Excalibur

"I look upon death to be as necessary to our constitution as sleep. We shall rise refreshed in the morning." ~ Benjamin Franklin

"Is he always this calm?" James asked as he examined Mercury. Running a close eye over the young, handsome buckskin's conformation and recognizing his bone structure and temperament, James continued, "Is this colt looking for a home?"

※
81

I suddenly felt an overwhelming swell of love for this young Mustang as I heard myself say, "No, he's actually coming to Colorado with me."

I was rather surprised that I had said that considering I never told this to anyone and, in fact, I didn't think I had really made up my mind to take him home at that point. But apparently, I did. I just hadn't gotten around to telling *me* yet.

What I didn't know was the day I made up my mind was the day he would die in my arms.

❊❊❊❊

It had been cold and rainy for the entire week and this January day was no exception. I had assisted and been present for many visits from veterinarians over the years. James, the vet, arrived at the barn, as he did so many times before, to examine and assist with a number of issues. We were preparing Mercury for what was supposed to be a routine gelding, and once he settled into the sedation-induced sleep, James began to "do the honors."

During the procedure my handsome Australian Shepherd, Merlin, who is very intuitive, continually asked to come into the stall and "assist." I told him to wait on the outside so that he didn't disturb Mercury and wouldn't get hurt should there be any unexpected movements. He left, but within a few moments, returned and laid down by Mercury's side. Once again I told Merlin to wait on the outside, this time reassuring him that Mercury was fine and he had nothing to be concerned about. So at my request, Merlin left the stall but continued to pace uneasily outside the gate.

After James finished the quick and routine procedure, we took a nice stroll down memory lane, passing the time till Mercury awakened. As James gathered his instruments, we realized that more time had gone by than was usual for a horse to be lying flat out. I mentioned my concern and James informed me that during the operation he had noticed that Mercury's inaugural rings, the entrance from the intestines to the testicles, were oversized. He said that this was something that could not have been determined until he actually performed the procedure and I should keep a close look out for any abnormalities as he healed from the surgery. If I were to see anything out of the ordinary I was to call him immediately. But a few moments later, none of that would matter.

We roused Mercury out of his very deep sleep. He raised his head and as he began to get up from the ground, my heart sank and the world turned up-side-down.

❊

As a former police officer, I was not what you'd call faint of heart. I had seen many things that would likely disturb the average person. For me it was just part of the job. But I was not prepared for what I was about to experience. As I looked at Mercury, his intestines began to flow out of his body like spaghetti. In seconds, they hit the ground. Tears began to pour down my face.

James ran to his truck to find the right tools. Pulling myself together, I radioed for back-up as the young colt ran into my arms. I cradled his head, seeing the fear in his eyes, desperately asking me what was happening. I felt helpless. I had no answers for him. In all the time I had cared for him I could always solve any problem he had. Now, all I could do was comfort this terrified horse dying in my arms.

As others came to help they could see the trauma written on all of our faces. James returned to the scene and told us he had no choice but to put Mercury to sleep. He had never experienced such a tragic castration in his career, but he knew there was nothing more he could do for the young colt. It all happened too fast. The only sign of trouble I had had was Merlin trying to tell me something was wrong. I just didn't understand.

✺✺✺

Several months later, my close friend was talking with Mercury. As an animal communicator, she was able to connect people with animals who had passed on to the other side, helping to heal the hearts of both. I felt the time had come to try to communicate with him.

As an animal communicator myself, I knew how to connect to him as well. However, it's common for animal communicators to consult colleagues when it comes to their own animals, as the strong emotions and desires can confuse or taint the information received, making it difficult to hear clearly. And that would have certainly been the case with Mercury. I didn't normally connect with horses in my care that had crossed over, but I needed to know he was OK. And I needed answers. Why did this happen? Why had he come into my life, only to be ripped away the moment I decided to welcome him in?

She immediately made a connection. He opened the conversation by saying, "I am not dumb!" I knew exactly what he was talking about, remembering when a friend of mine referred to him as such. This was the first piece of confirmation that we had indeed "found" my gentle colt. She continued receiving confirmation with details that she couldn't have known or guessed; things only Mercury and myself would have known.

✺

Then I heard something that both amazed and delighted me. Mercury said I wasn't ready for him. The time wasn't quite right for us to be together, but he would return to me in two years, when I *was* ready for him. He would come back as either a Gruella or a Buckskin colt and I would meet him when he was approximately nine months of age. Finally, he said he would be a Mustang, untouched, out in the pasture, and would have a dorsal stripe and three swirls.

I had been studying the impact of swirls for more than a decade with over 1,000 horses to date. Not only had it been proven that multiple swirls can indicate extreme personalities and intelligence, but it was also something I wanted in my horse, a secret I had told no one.

As Mercury, he was known to many to be pretty docile, but I had seen other sides of him – a curious, gentle side, and one full of beans, often kicking up his heals on our walks together. Now, with his return imminent, I couldn't wait to see what he'd be like the next time around.

※❖※❖※

In January 2007, I was invited to give a short speech at a local gathering, in support of the Mustangs, a cause dear to my heart. The meeting, a good two-hour drive from my home (one way!), would take place for a few hours in the evening. As I'm always pleased to be able to support and bring awareness to the American Mustang, I gladly accepted the invitation.

That winter was a rather unique one in Colorado. Living 9,000 feet in the foothills of the Rocky Mountains, we had record snowfalls. I stopped counting after about 18 feet of accumulation. Unbeknownst to me when I agreed to speak, the meeting would be postponed twice due to extreme weather conditions. With a very full schedule and travels that take me around the globe for 10 months of the year, this could have proven to be a difficult event to attend.

Finally, on the third attempt to reschedule the meeting I was unsure whether I wanted to endure over five hours of driving to give a 10-minute lecture, but, as I always honor my commitments, I decided to go.

I arrived in the cold and dark to an extremely warm and bright welcome. After meeting some very dedicated people, I gave my short speech and began preparing for my long drive home. I was asked if I would like to help feed the horses, but with temperatures at near freezing, I wasn't too keen to venture into the cold. I politely declined the offer.

A few moments later, one of the volunteers who did go out to feed came back inside. The ice cold weather was exacerbating her lung condition and she couldn't continue. She casually asked if I would go outside to assist, but, as most of the work was done, I felt there really was no need for me to help. So, again, I declined Eventually though, not being one who likes to sit idly by while others do the work, I decided to bear the cold and see if I could lend a hand.

I stepped outside to find that the young horses were already fed and in their pens. Sabine, who originally asked for my help, motioned for me to come and look at the young colts.

When I arrived, I was greeted by the eyes of a young colt staring at me. I could see his Gruella-colored head with a different colored body. I asked Sabine to encourage him to walk over to the light. As he approached, his cute Gruella head and buckskin body became clear in the light and, for the first time, I noticed three swirls on his forehead.

"This can't be happening," I thought, "It can't be him." Then I remembered that it had been exactly two years since Mercury's departure.

"This is Lancome," Sabine pronounced. Now intrigued, I noticed he had zebra stripes on his legs and a long, very obvious dorsal stripe with two stripes going over his withers creating the appearance of a cross. I immediately began to ask questions about the young guy, his history, his handling, but there was really only one question going through my mind – a question I couldn't ask.

He had come from the Spanish Mustang Registry in Oshoto, Wyoming where he was born and raised by his family on more than 4,000 acres. He was mostly unhandled, although sociable, classed as a Slate Buckskin and he was nine months old.

The most amazing piece of the puzzle was, just days before, I had called a couple of my friends and asked them to be on the lookout for a young Mustang colt giving this *full* description. I was ready to invite him into my life and here he was, standing before me. If the question was, "Is such a thing really possible?" the answer was staring back at me. The answer was, "Yes!"

I left feeling elated and confused all at the same time. Doubts began to slowly creep in. Was this real? Am I really ready for this guy? If I were to make this commitment, it would have to be for life or at least with the promise that I would do my best to honor him. As a clinician, traveling much of the year, I'd also have to find someone to care for him during my absence.

My prayers had been answered and yet I found myself questioning. I confided in a number of close friends and they all told me that this colt was "woven from the same cloth" as Mercury. There are only so many signs you can ignore before you have to take that leap of faith.

So on my birthday I invited "Excalibur" into my life. My husband and I decided to rename "X", as he is fondly known to us, choosing a name into which he could grow; one that would represent his strength and magnificence in years to come. He is now a very special part of our family.

What began as a simple acquisition of a favorite colt turned into some of the greatest lessons I have ever learned. Through his willingness to embark on the brave adventure from Mercury to Excalibur, by this one miraculous act, he showed me the meaning of sacrifice and unconditional love.

I experienced, first hand, that we can't control life as much as we'd like to think we can, and living in trust brings wonderful surprises – far better than what we could plan. But mostly I learned that miracles do happen. We just need to keep our eyes open and be willing to receive the gifts, however they may appear.

I am often asked what Excalibur's role is to be in my life and my response is always the same: "It's all up to him." If he enjoys the limelight, then he is welcome to assist me in educating the world on gentle communication. If, on the other hand, he prefers the quiet life, then we shall enjoy our time together naturally, wherever we may be. The choice is his… he's earned it.

Photo by Vincent Mancarella

Excalibur

Sam's Story

"Life isn't about waiting for the storm to pass.
It's about learning to dance in the rain." ~ Unknown

"How could he come back here after his wife and daughter were killed?" I admit that, perhaps, it wasn't the most positive and nurturing of thoughts, but it was the first one I had when I heard that Tom was repeating my natural horsemanship clinic. Although excited to see him again, I was somewhat apprehensive as to how, considering the circumstances, he and all the other participants would cope... how I would cope.

I was also concerned that a return to the same clinic would just be a tedious and, due to his recent loss, even painful repeat of last year for both Tom and his horse Sam. But I figured if he was willing to see what would happen, so was I.

I learned very early on in my career as a "horse whisperer", as it is so endearingly called, that true horsemanship is not just about information or training methods and techniques. That is merely the beginning, the surface of the vast ocean that is the relationship between horse and student. What anyone who is serious about horsemanship discovers is that the horse, more than almost any other being, is a mirror into our own inner selves. They read and instantaneously reflect our intentions, agendas, and emotions back to us.

You may be able to hide behind your smile, but you cannot hide behind your eyes. You can lie to yourself, and to other people, but you cannot lie to your horse. They see right through the lie and "feel" the truth.

If we are to touch that truth with our horses, we must begin with observing and listening, trusting our intuition, and developing that heart to heart connection. For, in every moment, our equine companions are speaking to us. Through their unspoken language, instincts, and family dynamics, we can learn a great deal from the herd.

By setting aside violent subjugation and working with compassion with our horses, we begin to uncover the hidden potential in ourselves and discover our own personal passions.

By allowing the horse to be the teacher, I discovered what Tom and Sam experienced changed not only their lives forever, but mine as well.

❖❖❖

At the beginning of the three-day clinic the year before, Tom had a big smile on his face. Even though he was a tall man, over 6 foot, his demeanor

❖

was welcoming and friendly. He told the group that he had been "dragged along by the collar" to the course and, despite his very limited experience, he agreed to come to support his beloved wife Janice in her hobby. So with her and her adorable, yet opinionated, Fjord pony, Sam, Tom began a very revealing three days.

One of the first of many exercises they tried was the Obstacle Course. Carefully chosen "obstacles" are placed around an arena, each one created to prepare a horse for what he might encounter every day in his life. A blue tarp was laid out to represent water crossings. A small jump was set up to teach him how to gauge correct heights. White chairs were lined up, forming a small, enclosed path, to help him learn to tackle small enclosures and alleyways with a relaxed and calm composure.

Along with a few other obstacles, the object of the exercise seemed simple enough; guide Sam through the course. But there was just one small catch – it was to be at liberty. In other words, there would be no physical contact with Sam, no restraints or physical aids. The only communication allowed would be visualization, energy manipulation, and body language.

I often use this exercise in my courses because it is a perfect introduction to the "language of Equus" and allows me to instantly learn about the individual relationship between the horse and his human. It also provides people with insights into their horse's personalities while simultaneously highlighting their own personal challenges and strengths.

Janice began by successfully directing Sam through the course, until she came to the alley of chairs. The strategically positioned white plastic chairs proved to be more of a challenge for her to negotiate. Sam didn't seem particularly concerned about the task, but he would conveniently avoid walking through the claustrophobic path, dodging the entrance at every attempt.

Many times people blame the horse when they come across a challenge. But in my experience there is no such thing as a "bad" horse. Horses learn through repetition, especially in three's, and when not clearly directed, they think they are faithfully doing what was originally requested. When we recognize that most equine-related issues are man-made, we can then approach the problem with a fresh, creative mind, addressing what we can do to help our horse understand exactly what we are asking.

Sam, like so many other horses, learned to take the path of least resistance, just as he also learned his other undesirable habits, through this misunderstanding.

So, I suggested it was a perfect time for Tom to join the exercise. He could help eliminate the optional avoidance routes by standing on one side of the chairs. Together, the two of them would clearly show Sam where they wanted him to go. But *the best-laid plans of mice and men often go awry.* Within seconds, Sam took charge of the new situation, highlighting not only Tom's horsemanship skills (or lack thereof) but also revealing a very clear picture of his personality and relationship with his human companions.

Sam strolled over with purpose, simply barging through Tom's attempts to block him. With every backward step Tom took, Sam just continued to raise his head high, presenting his powerful shoulder, and not missing a stride along the way. It was clear that Tom felt he did not have the ability to handle the situation. I attempted to coach him on how to physically and energetically increase his presence, but Tom didn't feel comfortable doing so.

On the second go around Janice was determined not to repeat the same mistake again. She recognized that their timing was off, but instead of communicating this to Tom, she immediately took charge of the situation to "save time and secure the *proper* outcome." She ran across to Tom's side of the chairs and began directing Sam, leaving her original position open.

"Guess who wears the trousers in our home?" Tom jested while Sam found a new direction to avoid the chairs.

I could see that Tom was struggling with the situation. But from his body language I knew that he didn't have an issue performing in front of others, nor did he lack the courage to easily complete the task. As a horsemanship teacher it is important to uncover the underlying issue in order to give the student the right tools to tackle the challenge, thus empowering him to succeed.

I considered the possibility that the difficulty was in Tom himself. That perhaps, his way of dealing with Sam was his way of dealing with other aspects of his life as well. Sam might, in fact, be reflecting back for Tom how he allows others to take advantage and overpower him. So, rather than assuming this was the case, I simply asked Tom if the scenario resonated with him in other areas of his life, and let him think about it for a while.

We then reevaluated and created a clear vision for the team. We didn't want Sam to learn he could push people around through shear strength and will power. Change was needed to avoid conflict and create success.

Together we came up with a new game plan. When Tom and Janice returned to the task at hand, they approached Sam with a new enthusiasm

⁂

and Tom seemed to exude a new sense of confidence. This time there was no question of what was being asked, and Sam responded as though he had walked the course his whole life. It appeared that clarity was all that was needed to set the situation right.

Through the rest of the clinic, Tom and Janice built on their successes and by the end everyone noticed a huge difference in their relationship with Sam. And Sam, previously labeled as an unruly horse, who came to the clinic feeling a leadership void, now left content, trusting his people to take the lead and take care of his needs. I was proud of all of them for achieving their goals and finding harmony. I felt that they had begun developing the foundation that would last them a lifetime.

❈ ❈ ❈

A few months later I received a message that broke my heart. Tom's wife and young daughter had been killed in an accident. In the blink of an eye, he had become a single parent with the responsibility of bringing up his sons. Faced with the greatest loss of his life, Tom was doing his best to create a safe and loving home environment while picking up the pieces of a shattered life.

With tears in my eyes, I told Tom that I was sending him and his family loving thoughts and prayers and, although I didn't mention it, I wondered what might become of Sam. It was a very real possibility, now that his wife was gone, that Tom, overwhelmed with the responsibility that had been thrust upon him, would have to give Sam up. I thought that might be the last time I would hear from either one of them again.

One year later, upon my return to Tom's home town, I was told that he and Sam would be attending the clinic again this year.

The clinic began, as it had the previous year, with introductions. Tom stood up and asked to share his personal story with the group. He began by recapping the tragic events that had so violently ravaged his life and, as we all did our best to hold back our tears, Tom told us Sam's story.

"Sam pulled the carriage with Janice's coffin in the funeral procession," he said. *"It was a sunny day, which was rare for that time of year. The children threw their shoes on the carriage to walk barefoot alongside the wagon."*

I noticed a spark in his eyes as Tom began to come alive.

"Sam had only ever drawn a carriage four times in his life, but he didn't miss a beat. With each footstep Sam took, he remained focused and determined to do his best. It was almost like he knew the exact route to take from the funeral home to the cemetery."

I could hear the pride in Tom's voice and I knew that Sam too was proud and that he had understood the importance of his role that day. Although unprepared himself for such an important event, in his way, Sam rose to the occasion. He took care of each and every member of his family that day.

I didn't want to interrupt Tom, but I needed to know why. Why did he come back? What could he possibly hope to gain by returning to the same clinic? Struggling to choke back the tears, I managed to get the question out, and this was what he said:

"Last year was such a precious gift for Janice and me. We found the spark in our relationship that had been missing for a long time. It strengthened our bond and enriched our lives together, even if it was only for a brief time. I want to relive that experience again with Sam."

During the clinic I was blessed to see the new relationship that had developed over the past year. No words could possibly convey the connection between them, the unspoken bond, and the depth of their relationship. They found solace in each other and Tom found what he had come to experience during the clinic. What I originally thought might just be a redundant and possibly heartbreaking experience, instead, allowed them to take the next step on their journey together. It was a sanctuary in which they deepened the bond that had been forged from tragedy, and strengthened their friendship between horse and human.

For me that weekend was challenging. There was certainly a whole lot I could have taught to Tom and Sam. But compared to what they both had gone through and what Sam taught me, the training itself seemed so very insignificant. This stout Fjord Pony managed to rekindle a relationship between Tom and Janice, help them grow as individuals, and bring comfort and unconditional love to his whole family... without doing anything other than being himself. In those three days, Sam reminded me that I can spend my time learning different skills, developing my expertise, and trying to better myself for an entire lifetime, but what matters most isn't what I can do or who I know, it is who I am in the world. Being me, expressing and sharing my authentic being, is the best gift I can give to the world. Something Sam does every day.

I would like to thank my co-writer, husband and partner, Vincent Mancarella, who often articulates my thoughts better than I do.

About
Anna Twinney

Anna Twinney is an internationally respected Equine Specialist, Natural Horsemanship Clinician, Animal Communicator, and Reiki Master. As the founder of the Reach Out to Horses® program she uses her unique approach, working solely in the horse's own language, teaching gentle communication techniques to create a genuine trust-based partnership between horse and human. Her interest in the "Language of Equus" has led her to focus increasingly on the power of animal communication to strengthen and deepen our relationships with all species.

Photo by Vincent Mancarella

For the Reach Out to Horses® Program, Anna has drawn on a lifetime of equine experience, over a decade of coaching more than 5,000 students from all over the world, and training over 1,000 horses, including the gentling of Premarin mares and wild mustangs for adoption and foster homes. Her expertise is sought by equestrian centers, trainers, managers, breeders, sanctuaries, therapists and amateurs alike.

Anna's lifelong love of horses blossomed early through her relationship with her childhood horse, Ringo, and then as an adult with Carrie, a Thoroughbred Irish Draught mare.

She began her exploration of natural horsemanship with Monty Roberts at the world famous "Flag Is Up" Farms. Anna, later decided to leave her career with the British police force and move to the U.S. in pursuit of her dream; helping horses and their people grow in partnership.

Returning to "Flag Is Up" she became an integral part of the research and development team helping to create and run numerous introductory and instructor courses, clinics, and exams for the Monty Roberts International Learning Center (MRILC). Qualified as one of the first six instructors throughout the world, Anna was the first to be entrusted with the title of Head Instructor at the MRILC and the only Head Instructor to be a member of the MRIA Board.

Anna has also worked in collaboration with other leading clinicians on natural horsemanship and animal communication. Additionally, she has explored a plethora of "alternative" healing modalities, including becoming a certified Karuna Reiki Master and Intuitive Healer. She has studied Equine Herbal Natural Remedies and Aromatherapy, is a certified Reconnective Healing® Level III practitioner and graduated from Carol Gurney's HeartTalk Program® as a certified animal communicator.

Anna's work has been featured in national and international magazines, newspapers and on television, including Martha Stewart's Living. She also writes articles for a variety of national and international equine-related magazines. She is the creator of the popular DVD series "Reach Out to Natural Horsemanship".

Anna's dream is to take the Reach Out to Horses® program around the world, especially to Third World countries, to make a difference in the lives of the working horses and people that are unable to travel to the U.S. One of Anna's great passions is the survival and protection of wild horses in the U.S. and around the world and she continues to support a number of charities and organizations in the hope that these majestic beings will be allowed to continue to roam free. For more information please visit us at www.reachouttohorses.com.

Whispers From a Horse's Heart: Four Lessons the Horses Have Taught Me

By Melisa Pearce

As I experience life and remain present to all the teachers within it, the learning unfolds. I suppose one grace of having endured a few decades is my awareness of the broad categories life lessons tends to fall into. I have discovered that there are four basic lessons that govern us in our attempts to remain authentic, and I am grateful that horses have worked as patient teachers with me, showing me these core messages again and again.

Lesson One: Show Up

When I was in the 6th grade, I began what would become a lifelong relationship with horses, thanks to my friend Shane, whose family lived on a small farm. Shane introduced me to horses and to riding. Riding his big sorrel gelding, Shane often ponied a small palomino mare to my house after school so we could ride along the nearby canal banks.

Some afternoons we rode out to the farm and it was on one of those rides that I learned the little gold mare was in foal. Shane's father announced that the vet had validated the little gold mare would be having her baby in five months. He wanted to make sure we started taking it easy on her and from that day forward, we only jogged and walked.

As 6th grade life dragged on, I watched the little mare become as wide as she was tall. A couple of months before her foaling date, I stopped riding her. Instead, I rode double with Shane and visited her as often as I was allowed to. I had no sense of what was involved in a mare foaling.

Twelve days past her due date, Shane was not in school. I was certain that meant she had foaled and I could not wait to call him after school to hear all the details. I called the farm several times, but there was no answer. The next day I waited for Shane at his bus stop. He arrived with his head down and with eyes swollen and red. The foal had died a few hours after its birth. I started to cry and felt completely lost as to what to say or do for Shane, let alone my little mare friend.

My mother agreed to drive me to the farm after school. I approached the mare not knowing how to act or what to say about her loss and sadness. She neither nickered to me nor jogged to the fence line to search my pockets for treats as she had always done before. Instead, she stood by herself with a flake of hay untouched at her feet, head hung low. Her white tail was matted with dark, dried blood and her back legs were stained with it as well. Her huge belly was smaller and her milk bag dripped droplets of milk on the dirt.

I opened the wooden gate and walked slowly toward her and ran into an invisible force field of sadness. It was as if a physical wave of sadness washed over me. Twenty feet from her, I was stopped in my tracks and began to cry. I stood there, frozen; until finally I wept the deep, full cry I had held in all day at school. Turning her small head toward me, she remained still and watched. After a few minutes, she gathered herself up and walked over to me and stood with the small white star of her forehead placed against my young chest.

My arms felt like lead as I stroked her face, hugged her neck, and shared that mourning space. I had no agenda that day. I needed to see her, connect with her, and experience my sadness with her. I don't know how long we stood there but I remember that we both felt a lot lighter when we were done. She returned to her hay and I to my home and bedroom to write in my journal.

That day I learned from the little yellow mare that the most important thing is to show up. Many times I have needed to break through my fear or my hectic schedule to do it, but she taught me to face everything, from grief to opportunities, by showing up. This may be the single most important lesson in a journey to be an authentic friend.

Lesson Two: Speak Your Truth

Many years later, my second child, Molly, was born. Her health and existence were in jeopardy from the day she was born, thanks to a rare disease. By age five, she had endured ten surgeries and too many nights in intensive care for me to count.

In between her hospitalizations, our family life was full and happy. I had my psychotherapy practice and enjoyed owning a small boarding farm. I loved caring for the boarders' horses as well as my own herd.

A month before Molly's fifth birthday, she took a severe turn for the worse and I spent forty-six days and nights never leaving her side as she slipped in and out of consciousness. It looked as if I was facing my very greatest fear: losing a child.

I had not been back to our home for over six weeks. When it was finally determined that Molly would be okay and would be able to return home in a few days, I was told to go home for twenty-four hours and get a taste of some normalcy. My stepmother stayed with Molly at the hospital and I went home.

Although mail was piled up and my bed and shower looked inviting, my heart wanted to go to the barn more than anything. I decided it would be my best medicine to go for a ride. I changed into riding clothes and walked out to the barn in the first sunshine and fresh air I had seen in weeks. Just beginning to reclaim a piece of myself again, I stepped into the barn aisle and, instead of being greeted by my dear friends, was shocked when, one by one, they moved swiftly to the back of their stalls, as if a cougar had just entered the barn.

Surprised by the reaction and tired beyond clear thinking, I was upset. As I approached the front of my pleasure mare's stall, she literally threw herself against the back wall and began to shake. I was certain that, in my long absence, someone – perhaps a barn cleaner or groom – had mistreated the horses. I stroked my mare's neck, attempting to comfort her and telling her that everything was okay. With a smile on my face, I told her I was home and would be sure to get to the bottom of it.

I continued to assure her as I haltered her. Placing her in the crossties, to stand on the familiar rubber mat, I went to the tack room to get a grooming kit. As I walked back toward her, she spooked severely in the ties and pulled back. This was a behavior she had never exhibited in all the years we had shown and worked together. I had raised the filly from birth and had owned her grandmother and mother. It was very disconcerting.

I took my time, brushing her and checking her out. I found no marks, cuts, bruises, or clues to her strange behavior. When I felt she was calm enough, I placed a pad on her and saddled her for a short celebration ride around the arena, in Molly's honor. The ride was the worst in my entire life. The bay mare continued to spook at everything.

Deeply disappointed, I gave up, un-tacked her, and placed her back in her stall. I decided to call the people who had been helping out while I was at my daughter's side to see if they knew what had happened. As I was walking back to the house, beginning to cry and feeling cheated of my precious healing sanctuary time with my horses, I was struck with the truth!

My body was filled to the brim with the fear that my child might die and even though my brain had begun to grasp the reality that she would live, my body and soul were still reeling with the vibration of terror. I had taken that smile on my face to the barn, but my best equine friends had sensed a much deeper reality in their alpha human. To my mare's credit, she had felt the real emotion in me and had begun to look for the predator that had me so frightened. The horses had never experienced me so lost and full of fearful vibrations. They sensed the incongruence between my words and what they were reading in my energy field.

I turned around on my boot heel with that awareness and returned to the barn, this time showing up in my truth. I stood at the edge of the mare's stall door and confessed how frightened I had been about Molly and that although the doctors now said that she had made it through the ordeal, my truth was that I was tired and my nerves were shot.

As I began to speak my truth, my mare relaxed and came over to the stall door. I opened the door and she welcomed me to cry upon her neck. She began to breathe deep, slow breaths and, together, we honored the truth . . . my truth. And that truth she could trust.

Lesson Three: Truly Listen

In 1989, I opened a retreat center on a summer ranch we owned in Flagstaff, Arizona. Our boarding farm ran well on its own and there was only a three-hour drive between the two places. I chose eight to ten horses each summer to take to the ranch, usually a couple of older trail horses and a few young ones I was working with for the show ring. Although our family and horses were delighted to escape the heat, my therapy clients were not overjoyed to have their weekly support and therapy sessions interrupted. By then I had been attending and facilitating retreats on borrowed properties for a few years and knew I could create a more powerful service for them at the ranch than they imagined.

I issued individual invitations to come up to the ranch for forty-eight hours at a time, in addition to several group retreat weekend sessions and workshops. I had set up a bunkhouse with its own kitchen, bedrooms, and bath. After the first month, my clients were all thrilled with the option.

We built two large yurts for additional meeting and sleeping space, an eight-stall barn, a hot walker, turnout pens, and an arena. The balance of the land was divided into two large pastures and the acreage was surrounded by Coconino National Forest, with unlimited acres of wooded riding trails.

The usual routine was for my clients to check in and get settled, then meet with me for a two-hour session midmorning. Then we met again for two hours mid-afternoon. This left both the client and me free for a few hours both days. Each client guest was encouraged to hike, relax in the hammocks hung in the trees, work with art materials I made available, spend some time in town, or otherwise enjoy themselves between sessions.

By midsummer, I began to sense that my clients were more centered when at the ranch and many clients shared that they were spending the time between sessions sitting by the barn, hanging out with a horse, or walking along the pasture fences. Some told me stories about how one horse or another had come over to them to hang out or how petting a horse's head had evoked their deepest tears and how touched they felt when the horse remained present instead of walking away.

That fall, clients often referred to their experiences with the horses. It was as if a moment with a 1200-pound animal had left an indelible impression they could still draw energy from when they needed to.

The next summer, I was ready to integrate some experiential sessions with the horses into my retreat and client sessions. Frequently, a horse exhibited behavior that the client saw as humorous or coincidental, like nodding his head up and down when the client spoke honest feelings or taking steps back away from the client if the client said something self-denigrating. We laughed and enjoyed the coincidences, and when I was alone with my herd, I thanked them for their incredible insight and loving expression with my clients.

As time went by, I realized how important these equine partners of mine were becoming. My partner horses were sentient biofeedback devices, lie detectors, and talented Gestalt therapy partners. All I needed to do was truly listen to their feedback. This became very clear in my work with Crystal.

Crystal had agreed to come up to the summer ranch once a month for three days to continue her work with me. She was a shy, sweet woman, neat and impeccable in her appearance. She had been working with me for only a few weeks before we began our summer routine.

Crystal was exploring her bouts of deep, and often suicidal, depression. Previous to our working together, Crystal had sought counseling from her church pastor and a therapist. Her family doctor had prescribed antidepressants. Nothing had worked.

After Crystal settled in, I gave her a quick ranch tour and invited her down to the barn. I introduced her to a couple of the horses who had not yet been turned out to pasture. Crystal had never been around horses and was hesitant to come very close, even at my encouragement. I noted how oddly aloof the horses were in her presence. They did not offer their noses, nor did they turn toward her. Once I had finished my morning chores, I released the horses to go to their herd mares.

Our first session delved back into where our work had left off and into Crystal's exploration of limiting beliefs. She had been raised in an extremely rigid family system. There had been behavioral expectations and a clear black and white way of viewing the world with very few chances for her to express herself or to develop her true self.

At the first break, I told her what time we would meet again and she went off to spend time on her own. I left to go saddle up for a long trail ride, which was the best way for me to clear my energy. I wanted to find a way to create enough safety for Crystal to explore her real feelings. The need for constant perfection and for rules, coupled with the fear of exploring what would make her happy, was causing her great pain. That pain locked inside her was immense and almost palpable, but there was also a rule that it was not acceptable to cry in front of others – not even her husband.

When it was time to reconvene, Crystal was ready, with a bare smile and a touch of color in her cheeks. I asked what she had chosen to do during the break and she reported that she had walked along the fence that ran beside the driveway pasture, looking at the horses. She had hoped they might come closer to the fence line and they had eventually grazed over to within twenty feet of her. They had mostly ignored her and, after a few minutes, had all left to continue grazing on the far side.

I first thought their behavior unusual because they often mooched face rubs from horse-experienced friends at the fence line. Curious, I asked her what she told herself about their behavior. She said that she knew she was an uninteresting person and it had felt familiar to be watching but not interacting with them. And for the first time, she allowed herself to admit aloud that she wanted that to change in her life. A tear leaked out from behind her eyes and slowly went down her face as she began to explore what she really wanted in her life and how much work it took to be so controlled inside.

The following morning, after I had completed the barn chores and turned the horses out for the day, my son's bay trail horse, Bueno, walked by my side all the way to the gate, as if he intended to follow me to the yurt where I was to have my session with Crystal. I stroked his mane and was touched he had chosen to walk with me. It was as if he had something to tell me.

Crystal was already in the yurt, looking fresh and rested. As she checked in, she reported that the sunset had been so pretty the previous night, she had gone down to lie in one of the hammocks next to a pasture fence. A horse had come over from the far side of the pasture to graze by her and she was surprised he had chosen to do that. She was even more surprised that he had stayed near her the entire time she was there.

On a pure hunch, I asked her if she would like to walk with me out into the pasture to meet and perhaps even pet him. She agreed, though she stuck close to my side as we entered the pasture. Bueno looked up as if expecting us and walked slowly toward us from the far side of the pasture. The rest of the herd also looked up for a moment, but then returned to their grazing.

Crystal was excited and affirmed that this was the horse who had joined her the night before. When Bueno came before us, he stopped about three feet from Crystal. This was not his norm. He was a kids' horse and was usually all over my son with his nose, searching for treats. He stood stone still, allowing Crystal to approach him at her own pace. I remained silent, curbing my desire to teach her about horses. Instead, I followed a voice deep inside me to just observe and listen to Bueno. He had somehow taken over the therapeutic session and was clearly in charge.

Crystal finally reached him and began to stroke his face and neck as he stood ever so still. Her body moved closer and closer until her arms were around his neck and he was able to gently cradle her by curling his big neck around her tiny waist. As he hugged her, Crystal began to shed a lifetime of tears into his neck, sobbing from deep within herself. The wise old horse's love poured into her as a much-needed release poured forth from her.

I was struck by the innate healing wisdom he had extended, in just the correct timing and with sensitivity to her needs. I thanked him later and told him I knew that such a big breakthrough could not have been made without him. I also knew I had just seen a glimpse of the shift my practice and work was about to make. It was a huge portal to the healing work I would co-create with many horses from that day forward. I learned that the better I truly listened to my equine healing partners, the deeper my work became.

Lesson Four: Don't Be Attached to the Results

In 2008, after almost two decades of equine work, I had just returned home from speaking at the Equine Extravaganza in North Carolina. My indoor arena and facility was prepped, cleaned, and set for the day's work. All ten horses had finished their breakfasts.

Rob, a referring therapist, arrived. He was to be co-therapist that day and had come early to bring me up to speed on the work he had been doing with the family that would soon arrive. The younger son was away in rehab and the family had been reeling from his discovered drug use. The older son would be present for the session and Rob had some concern that he was also using substances, even though there was no evidence of use and he denied it.

Rob wanted us to help the family release emotion and improve direct, clear, and honest communication between them. That was our agenda for the day. There was no expectation of big breakthroughs, just a desire to help the family release pent-up emotions about the younger son's drug use and begin to feel like a family again.

Once the family arrived and preliminaries were out of the way, I facilitated a check-in process, during which the family confirmed that none of them, but the son in rehab, was using drugs or alcohol, apart from the college-aged son's occasional beer.

I asked Martha to bring an older bay mare, Tory, out of her stall for a safety demo. With my assistants helping as safety aides, each family member became familiar with the horse and did some grooming as I evoked an emotional contact work experience with them. I moved through the first couple of hours layering the experience and gleaning what I could through the interactions.

Then I asked Martha to bring Thirty out of her stall and turn her loose in the sixty-foot round pen. The huge chestnut quarter mare had been with us for a couple of months to see if she could be a part of our healing herd. Thirty's owner had died of breast cancer the year before and she had been turned out with a band of broodmares after the loss. Her depression had lifted with our human contact, but she missed her herd of mares. It was unclear whether she wanted to do this type of work, but very clear that she was capable.

I asked Joe, the son, if he was willing to explore his energy in her presence. Compliant but ambivalent, he said he was and stepped up to the pen's entry gate. I gave him some of my observations, centered on what I had noted about the manner in which he "showed up" with his parents, and asked if he was willing to explore his interactions with others.

He agreed and stepped into the pen, fully expecting the mare to approach him. After several minutes, she walked over to him and ran her nose down to his left shoe, over to his right shoe, and back again. She cruised her muzzle up both of his legs and came to a pause at his belly. She remained there with her muzzle and then began to explore his hands. Joe opened the palms of both hands to her in silence. She scanned over them and ran her nose up both arms, not stopping until she came to his chest area. She stopped there and smelled him for a long time.

Joe's eyes began to moisten, and he wiped away a tear from his right eye. She then moved her muzzle to his throat and mouth as if taking in his breath, centering momentarily on his forehead. Then she ran her jaw line over the top of his head, knocking his ball cap to the ground. Thirty appeared to be reading and clearing his energy centers.

From just outside the gate, I observed the mare's work. I softly checked in with Joe and he reported he was doing fine. The mare stayed focused on her work and walked around behind him. I asked him to remain still. He nodded in understanding. Once behind him, she laid her broad nostrils on his back, where his heart center would be, and remained there for a long time. No doubt about it, Thirty was behaving like an equine Reiki Master, something I had not experienced with her previously. Then she took a small nip of his shirt and pulled him off-center on his feet and back toward her.

I bit my tongue and did not reprimand her for her roughness. I could clearly see that young Joe was taking it all in. Thirty then turned away from Joe and walked to the pen rail, as if dismissing him. Joe stood, puzzled by the interaction, and then began to nervously walk around the pen area. I asked him to check into his body and see if he was aware of anything. As he did this, Thirty licked the pen rails obsessively.

The horsewoman in me quickly made a mental assessment of the horse's behavior. I considered her diet, nutrition, and overall health. I could rule out the likelihood that she was satisfying a craving for a mineral in the metal. I then thought about the fact that I had never seen her have any stall vices that would lead me to believe this was a vice behavior. In the minute it took me to be certain of the feedback, I knew to trust that she was conveying information that she wanted me to receive on behalf of my client.

I refocused on Joe and asked him to check in to certain parts of his body and pay attention to his breathing. He reported that he felt good but tired. Thirty licked the bars harder and faster. The more Joe reported how well he was doing, the more Thirty licked the bars.

I thought about the desired outcome for the day: to facilitate a release of the pent up emotions. I had thought that Thirty was the horse who could assist this young man in doing this, and while she had already worked hard on his energy centers, he had done little more than shed a couple of tears. Yet the mare, in her wisdom and clairsentience, was not finished with him. She had an agenda beyond a bit of emotional release – one that would yield more profound results.

On a hunch that I understood her message, I asked Joe about his own involvement with drugs and with his brother's drug use. He denied any involvement. Thirty kept licking furiously. I brought his full attention to what Thirty was doing and asked him what he thought she was expressing. He said he saw her as a loving creature and believed she liked licking the bars. I told him that she called it as she saw it and was possibly demonstrating something she sensed was true about him. I asked if he knew what that might be. I explained that horses always told me the truth and asked if he had done the same.

This opened into a lengthy intervention and discussion, culminating in a release of pain as he admitted to having used drugs early that morning and to feeling responsible for getting his younger brother involved in the drug scene. This was the linchpin holding the family tension, and Thirty had just released it.

After many years of working with the horses who choose to do this work, I had known to listen to the mare and tease out the truth she was pointing to. But to do so, I had needed to remind myself to let go of all the desired outcomes and preset ideas about what we wanted to accomplish that day. It did not turn out the way any of us expected or desired on one level, but instead led to a much more important outcome for the family and Joe's mental health. It could not have happened without Thirty. We humans had come with an agenda and certain expected results. Thirty was wise enough to read the situation, instead of simply complying with the human agenda, and that had led to very different – and much more profound – results.

The beautiful chestnut mare had taught the fourth lesson in life: to never become attached to the results.

᠅•᠅•᠅

᠅

Through these four core lessons that the horses taught me, I have learned to be with others in an authentic manner. I am grateful beyond words for the patient way in which my equine guides have shared these truths. Regardless of the situation, I know I can draw upon these four lessons, picturing my blessed teachers in my mind as I come forth in a manner that never fails to support the greater good.

Blessed are those who experience the whispers from a horse's heart.

Gobar

My expressed gratitude to my mate Dane, who is on this life journey with me and our horses. Our horses are the dearest guides, most profound teachers and sweetest of all trusted confidants.

About
Melisa Pearce

Melisa Pearce, CEO of Touched By A Horse™, comes from an eclectic family background. Her Dad, a mechanical engineer, viewed the world as black and white, because to him, everything could be explained through physics. Melisa's Mom is an artist with a completely colorful view of the world. While Melisa learned to observe and experiment in the world like her Dad, and developed a heightened sense of imagination and inventiveness along the vein of her very creative Mom, her deep connection with horses came not from her family but from her own soul's calling.

Melisa's love affair with horses began when she was a young girl and laid the foundation for her modern day alchemy in weaving her years as an accomplished psychotherapist with her groundbreaking processes for working with horses and humans together in a therapeutic and healing way. Through the past twenty years of equine assisted therapy work, Melisa discovered she was able to bridge the human/horse species to form a space of energetic magic between the two. The combined creative energy allows deep and meaningful work to occur on heart issues, the chakras, and emotional and energy imbalances. All of Melisa's work is based in the horses' world of unconditional love and acceptance and their simple, elegant ability to be in the present moment with any person.

As an expert in human dynamics, a trained Gestalt psychotherapist, and a Master Coach, Melisa has taught a 400 hour Gestalt certification program and created her own method of Equine Supported Therapy and Coaching from a Gestalt Approach. Melisa found that the shifts people experience through working with a horse give them increased clarity and focus in their lives and help them to exhibit more determination and success in achieving their life's goals.

Chosen one of the Top 50 Most Influential Horsewomen by Horse South Magazine in 2008, Melisa has also won two World Championship

American Paint Horse Association awards. She has bred over 200 foals and managed multiple ranches while developing her expertise as a psychotherapist. Melisa is a gifted teacher who mentors students to follow her T.B.A.H.™ method through her Touched By A Horse™ Certification Program. She is also a Master Instructor for a joint venture company, and has facilitated retreats for executives, sales teams, families, and individuals for two decades. She has won the Editor's Choice Best Spiritual Retreat in 5280 magazine.

Melisa has been a clinician at Equine Affaire in Ohio and California and the Equine Extravaganza in Virginia and North Carolina. She also lectures nationally on Energy Fields and Horses and is an intuitive reader of horses. She is the author of *Whispers From A Horse's Heart*, a spiritually influenced card deck for inspiration, *Wisdom's Journey*, a guided 3-CD series to discover and create your future, and *Eponalisa, The Fall Ride, a Life's Purpose Parable.* When not traveling to speak about and demonstrate the powerful healing connection of horses and humans, she can be found on her Lil Bit North ranch near Boulder, Colorado.

Find more information about Melisa and her programs at www.touchedbyahorse.com.

Authenticity is a Big Red Mare

By Holli Lyons

The red mare could move with the power of her breed, with strength, agility, and grace. She was a big horse, in body and energy, with a huge head that in itself could be a very large and powerful weapon.

Brandy, my 5 foot 3 inch, 120-pound pregnant daughter, entered the round pen through the metal gate, moving away from the horse. The mare, at the withers standing 3 inches taller than the petite woman, slowly walked in my daughter's direction with her head down, and then stood beside her. As the soon-to-be mother walked around the pen, the mare quietly followed her movements, as if the horse were a protective shadow.

Brandy walked to the middle of the round pen, the safest spot for a participant. The mare continued to shadow her, softly and even reverently moving to the middle of the round pen as well. Then the mare lowered her massive head and touched her nostrils to my daughter's abdomen. The big red mare breathed quietly and softly as if taking away any fear on her intake, and breathing out confidence and a sense of safety. The mare's body continued to move almost snake-like, coiling around her as best a 1400-pound horse could. It was as if she were trying to surround Brandy's entire body, engulfing her with her immense presence.

My daughter had been around horses off and on since birth. At a very young age, she rode horses (with Mom or Dad's help), she walked around them without fear, and helped with the daily chores. Yet, due to my divorce and a change of living arrangements, Brandy soon left her association with horses, and not until she was nearly 15 were they back in her life. Of course at the age of 15, it was not horses that she was interested in. So to say the least, she was not familiar with horses in more than a passing association.

When it came to choosing an equine partner for the experience, Brandy had chosen a big, powerful horse, one who had endless potential to fulfill her breed's many purposes. Before entering the round pen, she stated her intention for the experience. "To be safe. I am nervous around horses and don't trust my ability to know what to do with them, and since I am pregnant, I just want to be in there and be safe and nothing else." As she entered the pen, my anxiety rose, as I knew that when it comes to horses, anything can happen.

The facilitator instructed her *not* to hide any fear, to remain congruent with her internal state, and to focus on safety as she turned and faced the big red mare.

From the outside it appeared as if the mare approached the pregnant belly acknowledging the living being within, and then moved in a safe and methodical manner to put herself between Brandy and any potential threat. The mare also kept her head down, putting herself in a vulnerable position for a horse, and an expression of equine body language informing Brandy that she had nothing to fear from the big red mare. The mare's movements appeared much like an embrace.

Outside of the round pen I wept. My big red mare had become the small, soft, and gentle protective blanket of comfort that my daughter had asked for. They stayed in their intimate embrace for the rest of the experience. "How beautiful," I thought, feeling very blessed to have witnessed the mare in such a nurturing way, as well as believing that Brandy had experienced something quite profound. She had felt safe.

We had learned of her pregnancy the morning of the workshop. Not knowing what the activities were ahead of her, before going into the round pen, Brandy was nervous. Yet when it was her turn to choose a horse for the afternoon experience, she chose to be in the round pen with the big red mare. She explained that they had made a connection in an earlier observation activity. "When we walked around and looked at each horse, I just got a calm feeling around the mare, and the thought, 'I understand' came to me. So I chose her for the afternoon round pen experience."

Later Brandy described her experience. "I remember...(the mare)... following me slowly as I walked around the pen, just being with me, and at one point, walking straight toward me from across the pen, putting her head down and nuzzling my arm and hand... I felt completely unthreatened and safe the whole time. I also felt comforted, like she was saying, 'It's OK'. I wasn't afraid or nervous like I often am around horses."

Brandy's equine partner was a Hanoverian, a German Warmblood mare. Warmblood horses originated from crossing the hot blooded, high spirited Thoroughbred or Arab breeds with the colder blooded, slower moving, working breeds such as Belgians, Percherons, or Clydesdales. At 16.2 hands and the body mass of the working breeds, the big red mare looked more like the older style Hanoverian. In body size alone she was a big horse. Her hot blooded breeding contributed qualities such as grace, reactive speed, and alertness, providing this mare with potential for a highly energetic presence.

Warmbloods were bred to be a level-headed, easy to ride, versatile mount. They not only had to be able to plow the field and carry their rider to town, they also needed to be the war horse that moved with agility to save the warrior from his enemy by rearing and taking the blow, by maneuvering quickly out of the way, or by speeding off out of range. They represent the majestic, powerful, well-rounded and balanced equine; just like the big red mare that shared a round pen with Brandy that warm July day.

✳✳✳

In my work facilitating personal growth and awareness training programs with horses as my co-facilitators I have noticed some participants have what they call "big energy," a phrase that they used when describing themselves. "Big energy" in their case meant people who commanded attention. They did this by being more vocal, by their actions, or quite honestly, just by their energetic presence. They came to be this way via different sets of circumstances, yet when they were in a room everyone felt it.

During various programs the "big energy" participants expressed that they had expected to come to the training and be automatically accepted for who they are. They expected to be able to express their bigness without any pressure to reel it in, and to feel safe to be their energetic selves. Yet they voiced that there were incidents when they felt they were being asked to hold their energy inside and could not always be themselves. They felt they were being asked to change for other people. They felt frustrated and questioned what was "fair."

During these same programs there were other participants who fell to the other end of the spectrum; people who were highly sensitive, who during their normal lives encircled themselves with a protective bubble keeping the unsafe world outside; people who felt that they could not show their true selves to the rest of the world without being judged as weak, too sensitive, or becoming vulnerable to outside energies. They were expecting to come to the program and be able to allow their sensitivity to blossom, to develop their intuitive natures, and to practice energetic expansion.

✳

They expected to do this in a safe environment. Yet when confronted with peers who needed to have a place to express their bigness, to show their true energetic presence, they felt attacked and the opposite of safe. They felt they were being asked to reel in their energetic sensitivity, to stay hidden, or to not show their true selves. They too felt frustrated and questioned what was "fair." How can both survive, thrive, and develop during the same program, on the same farm, or even in the same universe?

Each participant struggled with their chosen identity, as well as group dynamics. There were conflicts, resolutions, and change. My association with these powerful and amazing personalities led me to a profound awareness generated partially through the conflicts they generated. Without these experiences, which were not always pleasant, I would not have learned the lessons I needed to learn. My deeper understanding of the concept of authenticity was ignited by my association with these powerful and amazing personalities – and further fueled by my big red mare.

At home one crisp, sunny fall day while watching the big red mare, enjoying her powerful presence and her sometimes flamboyant bigness, it occurred to me how she was just like the participants in the trainings. Here was this presence that not only was physically big and powerful, she also emitted expansive energy whenever she had the opportunity to move as she was *meant* to move. I simply was in awe of her whenever she presented herself in all of her bigness and equine power. Yet she was also a highly alert, sensitive, and reactive horse, aware of every external stimulus. She was the one who would spook at nothing, the one who alerted the herd of any potential threat, and the one who required an extremely quiet and gentle hand when ridden. Here was a mare that could in one moment be big energy and the next require the softest, lightest touch; a being who intuited intention and responded as required.

My thoughts went back to that day when the mare was in the round pen with Brandy. I remember how small the horse had become. How her energy had been pulled back into her body, not out of shame, guilt, or fear, but out of knowing what was needed in that particular moment, for that particular experience. She knew what was needed for the "herd" to be safe. She had become a small, soft, and nurturing energy, not any less than what she was when she exuded her big, powerful energy; simply different.

The big red mare modulated her energy by being fully present in the moment, by not engaging any ego driven rules of behavior, and without becoming less than who she was. In fact, she had become more in that moment with Brandy: she had become the protector, part of the same sisterhood, part of each other, expanding the connection outside the realm of species. Had I mentioned that the big red mare was also pregnant during that round pen experience with Brandy? They were sisters in the continuation of life, in the world of the ultimate feminine.

This big red mare is always true to her nature, always true to whatever is going on inside of her in the moment, and is never worried about what someone in the environment might think of how she is acting. She never diminishes her powerful essence by her actions. She is willing to express her enormous energetic presence, and willing to become small and soft, containing her energy within. Yet when her energy is contained within, it is not shackled and held against its will struggling to be released. It is peaceful and content, available should it be summoned.

Additionally, the big red mare is constantly sensing what is going on around her. She sensed Brandy's state of mind, emotions, and energy level at every moment. She embraced the sense of peace and need for quiet safety. She watched Brandy's body language and she felt her breathing. She felt the second energetic presence within Brandy and responded to the needs of the moment. She did not question what she sensed, she simply went with it. She did not care that we watched, nor was she worried about what we might have thought of her. She acted authentically to what she was presented with in that moment, willing to change responses in the next.

I have used this story in the past whenever I am presented with a situation concerning the powerful feminine and reclaiming the feminine warrior spirit. The big red mare has always represented to me the power of the feminine, the ability to nurture, as well as to be all that one can be. The ability, in any single moment, to reach into our natures and pull out the power needed at that particular time. Yet only recently did it occur to me that this is also the perfect story about being true to your authentic nature, the ultimate picture of a balanced being.

Now, whenever I think of authenticity, I think of the big red mare. She does not compromise herself by her actions, but rather creates a more complex and versatile self. Each authentic action creates another option in her repertoire of experiences to tap into for the next situation that arises to maintain her personal safety, that of the herd, or to synchronize with another, as she did with Brandy.

I have seen this mare, in similar situations with clients, pace back and forth, swishing or wringing her tail anxiously, glancing only briefly at the client, constantly vigilant to what is going on outside and never relaxing enough to stand beside the person in the round pen with her. I have seen the same mare follow a client, head down, mirroring each and every movement, yet sending the message of connection, not safety. I have seen this mare run frantically around the pen, unable to get her energy to the point of walking and being close to the client, only able to experience the anxiety of the moment and to be in constant motion, ready to leave if the opportunity were to present itself. I have seen this mare kick with glee and present her full range of athletic abilities as the client, smiling, watches in amazement and awe. Unlike most humans, the big red mare does not hold onto who she was yesterday, or plans who she wants to be tomorrow; she is who she is in the moment, ready to change as the situation demands and her authentic nature perceives.

I have observed myself in situations where I have learned to pull back any energy that I could call me, and to place myself into the role of total observer rather than participant. I did this as best as possible at the time, allowing that I am getting better at it as time and opportunity are presented. I call this practicing the art of invisibility. I have summoned my energy to become bigger than life when the geldings have raced to the gate at dinner time sure that they each should be first through the gate to get to their food. I guess if I were to give this a name also, I am practicing the art of becoming the dragon; stopping the onslaught and clearing the path with one breath.

⁙⁙⁙

Ideas and concepts evolve over time. The horses teach us what we are ready to learn and only when we are ready. Ideas about energy, learning to modulate it, how it can affect others, safety, and more than I can list, have presented themselves to me during various programs. These experiences have helped me to formulate a fundamental concept about authentically owning and using personal power.

Everyone comes into this world with infinite energetic power. Your task is to learn how to claim the greatness that you are, flow with the current moment experience, and be all that you can and are meant to be in *this* moment. By not allowing the ego to limit the endless possibilities available, you summon your personal power, focusing it internally or externally depending on the need from moment to moment, situation to situation and goal to goal. Just like the big red mare demonstrates when she summons enormous energy at feeding time announcing her position as first in line or she morphs into plush-like energy as I massage her ears.

⁙

Authenticity has more than one side. The big red mare exemplifies being authentic; being what is real or natural. She demonstrates the ability to switch from being bigger than life to becoming almost invisible depending what the moment reveals. The mare does not become something that she is not. She draws upon the multi-dimensional being that she is.

Then there is the other side of authenticity, the receiving side, being willing to accept what is authentically offered each and every moment without judgment, without expectation, and without holding on to the past or future. Allowing for the other, whether human or equine, to express their own authentic nature in each moment. We must respond with the fluidity of the horse, sensing the authentic action based upon the action of the other. In this way, being and allowing, a natural flow, an authentic relationship, or an authentic exchange is created.

I remember one situation during a workshop where a "big" energy female participant was in a session with a cold blooded Percheron gelding, a large white horse that normally was hard to get to move and knew how to stand his ground. Yet as the participant opened the gate to the arena, the enormous white gelding ran to the other end. He paced frantically and at one point actually stood on his hind legs as if he was ready to hop over the railing. All of this while the participant was still at the other end of a football field sized arena. I was shocked, yet knew for him to act that way that he must be responding to a very strong presence. Here was a 2000 pound animal that normally needed a great deal of encouragement just to put one foot in front of the other. Wherever the woman moved, the gelding moved in the opposite direction and stayed as far away from the participant as he possibly could.

The facilitator brought the horse's exaggerated reaction to the participant's attention. She mentioned the possibility that perhaps the participant's energy intensity might be a factor and suggested that the participant play around with modulating energy levels; taking her energy down and bring it back up in a controlled manner. In this particular case, the participant's energetic level was so engrained that she found it difficult to make even the slightest modification. The participant finally acknowledged that she just did not know what to do. As soon as the woman voiced her state of not knowing, the large white horse immediately slowed down his pace and was eventually able to come to a halt. He still did not become the calm, quiet, statue-like being he normally was, yet he was more earthbound. He had responded to the woman's authentic awareness of her internal state in her moment of frustration and confusion.

The "big" energy woman had not made a significant change in the bigness of her energy; she had allowed herself to witness the response of the horse when she acknowledged her state of being, what she was experiencing in that moment. The horse was able to respond positively to her authentic not-knowing, yet needed to also hold onto his authentic concern. I was reminded that you do not necessarily need to change anything. However, you do need to become congruent, matching your external actions with your internal state. This is part of developing awareness of how individual energies interplay so that you can make conscious choices. Your authenticity does not live independently of others.

When we do not have attachment to what occurred seconds ago and are willing to experience and feel only what is happening in the moment – that is being authentic. When we are not attached to outcome or any agenda, we are being authentic. This does not mean responding in a vacuum without concern for others we may affect. This is responding to everything and *all* things; yet only to what is true and real in *this* moment.

❊❊❊

Now as I think back to events during the various training programs, the many sessions with the big red mare, as well as the concepts of being in the *now* and non attachment, I realize the simplicity, yet at the same time complexity, of authenticity. Sometimes when we feel the freedom to be ourselves or have a profound experience of self-discovery, we try to hold onto that feeling or experience. The original feeling or experience is authentic; trying to hold onto it past its point of realness requires forced action, which is not authentic. This forced action requires a great deal of energy and does not allow for other authentic actions or feelings to occur.

Our honest sensitivity to the present moment is dulled and colored by bringing the past and sometimes future desire into the picture. What is truly trying to occur, the authentic action, is sabotaged by our holding onto our memory of what we think we want. Horses, on the other hand, are willing to change action or direction based upon the results of their actions.

In another situation, a "big" energy participant was about to enter a round pen with a small black mare. In previous sessions with different horses, this participant had experienced difficulty modulating her "joy" whenever she was asked to move a horse. Her excitement would go from zero to sixty in an instant, resulting in the horse racing around the round pen unable to find a quiet, neutral spot.

Upon being asked the intention for this session, the participant said, "To have an authentic relationship with this mare." The woman entered the round pen remaining conscious of her intention. The horse began to move off and then stopped, turned, and looked at the participant. The facilitator suggested that the participant periodically check in with her body and with the mare by asking herself what she was feeling and what was occurring in that moment. Whenever the participant did her check in, the mare would move in closer to the participant and mirror whatever movement the participant was making. Whenever the woman got excited and began to dissociate with her joy the mare would move away. By the end of the session, the smiling woman and small black mare were moving in unison as if they were one being. "I have never had such an intimate experience," commented the participant as tears were wiped away. Observing the experience I noticed how my own body relaxed and felt peaceful by the end of the session.

Trying to hold onto a set way of being, such as "bigness" or "sensitivity" does not allow for other ways of being or other experiences. It can feel so good to be able to express who you "really" are. Yet, trying to sustain what felt good in one situation and transfer it to other situations does not end up feeling good all the time. It may not be safe for you or others. It may not be authentically what you feel or who you are in the new situation. Yet you want to hang onto that "good" feeling; sometimes even when at this moment you are not feeling all that good. Being able to appreciate the current experience can be learned. It is something that becomes more natural and easier for you as you allow yourself to live in the moment, to become more horse like.

A primary driving factor for the wise horse is to conserve their energy. They graze or rest the majority of their time. They do this so that at any moment, if and when a burst of speed is required, they have it in reserve. When that crouching mountain lion, hungry and on the hunt, laying low in the grass, creeping ever so quietly, is ready to pounce, the wise horse has the speed and energy available in a split second to out run the attacker. Horses do this with the energy they have conserved being who they are, being wise, and being authentic. They are sensitive to *now* and what is needed in the now. They do this without attachment to what was a moment ago, nor have any attachment to what is in the future. They do not judge the mountain lion for being a mountain lion. Nor do they waste energy wishing they were the mountain lion or that there weren't any mountain lions. They eat grass, they run, they stop, and then they eat grass.

Following the easiest or most natural path and living in the current moment supports the agenda of the horse to conserve their energy for when it is needed. This energy can be used to run from a predator, play with a buddy, or move to a better grazing spot. Horses work together as a team. They move in ways to protect the safety of the entire herd. They do it the easiest way possible. They follow the natural flow, allowing emotions to come and go, flamboyant expression to have its time, and then not. They spend most of their time enjoying each other; kicking up their heels when they feel like it, being quiet and alert when the lead mare signals, and going back to grazing as a cohesive group when all the fuss is over.

If I have learned anything from the horse, it is to let go of past action, allow my self to be what wants to be *now*, while at the same time willing to put my head down and munch away, swishing my tail in contentment, grazing with friends and family, sensing the authentic action for this and only this moment. That is authenticity. Just like the big red mare.

The Big Red Mare

With gratitude and love I thank my family, Don, Brandy, Erin, Noah, Matt, Isabella, Makena, and Paige for their endless support and encouragement on my miraculous journey. Their presence in my life is my greatest inspiration, as are all of the wondrous horses living in this world or the next who have graced me with their kinship and wisdom.

Authenticity is a Big Red Mare
By Holli Lyons

Born with the spirit of the ancient equine,
tapping unlimited potential.
Embracing each moment with its uniqueness
The Big Red Mare grazes.

The power and bigness reside inside
always present, available when needed,
yet never summoned without peace beside.
The Big Red Mare breathes in, then out.

Pure in her intention.
Free with her emotions.
Concerned for the safety of all
The Big Red Mare does no harm.

She is always who she is.
Never less than who she can be.
Willing to get big enough to become invisible,
The Big Red Mare observes.

Aware only of the moment.
Concerned with what wants to happen.
Never worrying about what could be,
          what might be,
                    or what should be.
The Big Red Mare follows the natural path.

She plays and eats in her own time.
Willing to rest and conserve.
Knowing when the mountain lion chases,
The Big Red Mare's energy is in reserve.

She never runs all day; exaggerating or forcing.
Such effort can not be sustained.
She flies when it is time to fly.
The Big Red Mare is one with the Way.

About
Holli Lyons

In the fall of 1999, Holli Lyons became the guardian of an amazing Hanoverian stallion, Europe. Her relationship with Europe became the catalyst for her journey and exploration into all things equine.

Knowing that a stallion requires advanced horsemanship skills, Holli studied Natural Horsemanship at the Parelli ranch in Colorado with Pat and Linda Parelli. She realized establishing an independent seat was critical and studied Centered Riding with Karen Irland and with Mary Fenton. Her journey took her to New Mexico, studying Feldenkrais with various teachers and especially Rahina Friedman who transitioned Feldenkrais onto the horse's back. At home she became acquainted with the Alexander Technique. Trips to Washington State introduced her to Joseph Freeman, where she studied Equine Natural Movement, body work for horses.

Along the way she read Linda Kohanov's books, which led her to Linda's ranch at Apache Springs outside of Sonoita, Arizona where she studied and became an Advanced Instructor in Equine Facilitated Experiential Learning. Her work with Linda, Kathleen Barry Ingram, and Shelley Rosenberg changed Holli's focus. She established Breathe In ~ Breathe Out @ Lyons Gait adding EFEL to her small Warmblood breeding operation.

Holli offers workshops, group or individual sessions, and customized intensives at Lyons Gait or at her client's sites. In 2009 she added an EFEL Apprenticeship program, providing training, awareness, and experiences for those interested in bringing EFEL into their work with people or horses. Sessions with horses offer clients opportunities to experience alternative and sustainable life options in areas such as leadership, parenting, creativity, intuition, being in the present moment, empowerment, and communication.

Holli's journey sidestepped several times. One side path took her to the Process Work Institute in Portland, Oregon. Holli found the Mindell's process-oriented psychotherapy approach complimentary to the work she does with horses. Each focuses on the client being the wisdom keeper, the knower, and allows the process to unfold naturally. Discovery is brought into the client's emotional and body awareness so that old patterns can be exchanged with new and desired ones that the client has experienced during their sessions.

The most recent side path Holli has taken is in the area of spirituality. Eternally a student, Holli studies Buddhism, Taoism, and Shamanism, to name a few. For Holli, the natural aspect of spirituality is represented gloriously in the horse. She has taken this concept and infused many programs she offers with teachings from nature.

Holli has a BA in Management and Organizational Leadership. She lives with and is emotionally supported by her husband, Don, various cats, dogs, horses, children, and grandchildren in Northwestern Oregon. Spending 26 years in the electronics industry (sales, marketing, and management) provided many leadership, travel, and educational opportunities. Her husband, also having many years in leadership, jokes that they utilized these same leadership skills and methods raising their three children – or perhaps it was the other way around – they used their parenting skills in their leadership roles. Her website is www.lyonsgait.com.

Teaching the Wisdom of the Horse Ancestors

By Wendy Golding

I am Thor. Like the power of my new name, the God of Thunder, I fly as if through the heavens, with my feet striking the stars as I travel between worlds. My sleek, black, enormous body is filled with the sheer joy of being in this perfect moment of unity with everything in my universe. I leap and prance, my tail upswept as excitement flows through me. I am here, eager to share my story of how I came to be a teacher of humans.

My hooves pound the earth, filling me with self-satisfaction, grounding me with delight. Clods of earth fly through the air as I traverse the meadow, galloping across the green field. My forelock tangles with my long mane as the wind joins me in my dance of power. I am filled with glory, with effortless movement from all of my muscles working together to form a beautiful union of body and soul. My heart beats in unison with the smooth movements of my body. I could run on and on, and on.

My senses come alive, my skin quivering with excitement as I take in everything around me simultaneously. Out of my right eye, I see the tall, majestic guardian trees welcoming me to this place that is filled with serenity and healing energy. To my left is a large, gray, weathered barn, the stones in its foundation filled with the history of the ancients. I sense the movement of a leaf as it floats by on the cusp of an air current. The air is clean as it enters my nostrils, the strong, spicy aromas of manure droppings combined with the moist earth that was recently kissed by the rain, and the succulent grasses waiting to be grazed.

With my acute hearing, I hear the nicker from nearby horses. Crows caw their greeting as I touch the earth. There is a deep connection with all things. My body bursts forward, hooves hitting the ground as I run freely. I revel in all my senses as I gallop down the long fields of my new home.

Brasita greets me. The first mare to approach me, she is fascinated by my sheer size and presence. Dancing hesitantly toward me with her ears rapidly flicking back and forth, she stops short and races back to her horse companions. Lady, the lead mare, sends Brasita back to me, although Brasita doesn't need another invitation. We have already recognized each other as old souls sharing the wisdom of our ancestors.

As I stand in place, each horse comes to investigate me. Angelina expresses her concern that I will take over the role of her male, Monty. She shows her disdain by pinning her ears back, shoving her nose at me, and acting haughty. Monty, the lone gelding, demonstrates his stallion energy by rearing and squealing at me. Maintaining my calm demeanor, I send him a message that I support him as he holds the space of great wisdom for the herd at my new home.

This new place feels different than my previous home. When I stepped carefully off the trailer, my feet touched the earth and it sang to me of peace and healing. My new caretakers have created a sacred space where we are empowered to interact with and teach humans.

Here, I can just be a horse – respected for my natural strength and beauty, and my wisdom. Here, I can say *no* if someone wants to touch me or if I don't want to do an activity. Here, people wait for *me* to invite them closer or for me to approach them. I choose whether to engage or not.

My herd mates helped me learn about this new way of being around humans. Using long forgotten knowledge and wisdom, they call to people in their dreams, birthing a deeper part of themselves so they too can feel a profound connection with life.

On this sunny day, I am led toward a big covered space, moving from the warmth to a cool, bright open area. Inside the large pen, I feel nervous. Taking my halter off, my caretaker allows me to move freely on my own. I sense many horses having traveled here. As I explore this quiet place where bars restrict my access to the open area beyond the pen, she stands still in the center of the pen and watches me as I sniff the delicious smells coming from the earth.

I become aware of her relaxed body as she slowly approaches me. Sensing my energy field, I hear her breathe in deeply and see her rock back slightly. My ears flick ever so slightly and my breathing calms. As she starts to come forward again, I slowly turn and approach her. Letting me draw near, she patiently waits. I am confused because she doesn't touch me. This is strange. Humans usually touch me on my face where I can't see. Instead, she moves to stand calmly next to me, her shoulder next to my shoulder. I relax. It feels good. I sense a harmonious connection growing between us. This is my first of many healing experiences in my new home.

Upon returning to my herd, the horses whisper that we are teachers to humans. I am amazed, yet mystified. I am used to doing what humans want me to do – unquestionably. I am confused. How can this be?

One by one, the other 10 horses share their experiences with humans and how each of their special gifts is honored. The horses teach me how to open my heart to the horse ancestors who share the wisdom of our species. When I access this ancient knowing, I see images of horses and humans, linked over thousands of years. Our two species are intertwined, and by working together in this new way, humans are becoming more aware of a higher consciousness. Connecting intentionally with the wisdom of many past horse spirits – especially the horse warriors – I share their collective knowledge with the humans who come to discover this awareness.

The horse warriors of past ages encourage me to teach people to find the courage to take that first step into a place of infinite peace as we connect to all things. Using this guidance, I spark a human's awareness by just being. A sense of calm prevails as I stand next to a person. My heart energy seeks to connect to the person's heart energy. I can see the person energized for a second and then they relax and breathe in unison with my breath. Their mental busyness shifts lower into their chest, into their gut. I can feel a settling as they connect their mind, body, and heart as one.

How do horses connect with humans? Let me explain in human words. A thought becomes a visual image in my mind. Communicating this way helps me focus my intent. When the human is in a place of openness, they can feel my message, interpreting my language by intuiting the information through their senses of hearing, seeing, and feeling. Horses naturally use this as part of our language; we communicate telepathically with one another. I can't hold a thought very long yet, but the sensations or residue from the communication have a lot of impact on the humans.

How humans respond to the message is interesting. Sometimes they feel an emotion welling up; sometimes a sense of peace and well being; some actually hear my message.

Feelings are the key. Emotions are crucial information for our survival. As horses live by our instincts, we are very sensitive to our environment and all those who come in contact with us. We experience an emotion, take action, and go back to grazing. Emotions and experiences are just information that we process and let go. Emotions equate to energy in motion that ignites our cellular activation. We can read this activation in ourselves and other horses and humans, like reading a book of impulses that travel from the heart, to the brain, to the gut, and back.

We horses have enormous circuitry going through our intestines. Through this circuitry, we are very sensitive to currents of energy that flow through us to the person we are connecting with. These electrical impulses can be fast or slow, spiking or calm.

Our energy field is intertwined with the human energy field. There is a common harmonic evidenced by the strength and closeness of the horse/human bond traveling through thousands of years. In the universe, there is a single, unified system of nature connected through a vast, ancient web of energy. Through the open expression of our emotions, horses are in tune with this pulsing, resonant field. Our field of energy provides a container and a bridge for humans to sense everything that is happening between the world within and outside their bodies. As the horse/human energy fields intersect and merge, the human may sense a feeling of well-being, without knowing what it is attributed to.

When we teach a human how to be present, the person experiences an awareness of our ancient language. It is a way to "just know" something. I am excited as we all learn together how to expand this new way of non-verbal communication. The more I use my abilities with humans, the stronger my link of connection, opening more opportunities for learning and expansion.

I especially enjoy it when I am able to teach the people how to become aware of our energy so they become much more in touch with their own energy. What I have come to understand is that in their busy lives, people are not in touch with the feelings in their bodies. I am aware when a person begins to sense the waves of energy my body is emanating, vibrations created by my electromagnetic field. When that happens, I wiggle my ears or move a part of my body. The closer they move to my body, the more conscious the person is of my strong energy. They might even feel a tingling in their hands or warmth in their chest.

In this type of interaction, people are relating to me from the ground. Opening to the connection, I sense their rate of breathing, the beat of their heart, the muscle tension in their body, the smallest of their actions, their unique smell, and the cadence of their voice. Instinctively, I find that one piece of information the human needs to change in the moment to achieve a better balance between their body and their mind. Acting out my feelings, I reflect back to them the information they require.

My first experience with people other than my caretakers is an equine facilitated learning workshop. One woman in particular is drawn to my gentle male strength. Her story of early male abuse touches my heart, and

I feel a desire to show her that male power does not need to be abusive. I gently place my nose on her chest and as we softly breathe in and out in unison, a wordless connection touches her deeply at her core. She finally accepts and opens herself to the strong energy of the male or yang connection within herself that she has rejected for so many years. We both are healed by the simple unity that exists between all things.

The next activity the woman introduced me to is the Boundary Dance. She walks gently on her feet as she comes close to me. I move slightly away, and the woman stops and takes a breath, then starts walking gently forward again. She can sense where I am comfortable having her stand in relationship to my body. Slowly lifting her hand to my neck, she places her hand firmly on my skin and allows it to rest there before she gradually strokes the skin on my neck. Ripples of pleasure move through my muscles. Leisurely she moves her hand up to my face. That doesn't feel as nice and I back off slightly. She respects my need for more space and continues to just be in my proximity.

If I move abruptly, my huge male presence seems to trigger something, and her body quivers in fear. By breathing slowly and deeply, she reconnects to her body and mine. Finding her place of power, she sets a firm boundary, asking me not to approach any closer. I gently respond to her request and respect her wish. Feeling empowered, she invites me closer and we again feel that connection of unity.

During this and other spiritual workshops, I am encouraged to further open my heart to access the wisdom of my species and align it with the humans' species wisdom. Within months, I learn to recognize which person is best for me to help that day. I read their body language; how tense they are, how fast their heart beats, how they carry themselves, how their voice sounds to my ears. From those cues, I connect with the person and communicate my willingness to work with them.

Being with a person while they try to "lead" me, I respond to what their body is saying, the noises they are making, their overall energy, their heartbeat, and their breathing. If they are connected to their inner self, I feel safe to be with them, and I willingly follow them. As their posture and breathing changes I can feel that they are more grounded and centered, and know they can walk this new way of being in their everyday life.

Watching a group of people try to move me is funny. They don't know how to use their energies as one. In my herd, we are so sensitive to one another, that if we sense something dangerous, we turn as one herd and run away from the danger. We feel an energetic impact or wave of energy

... in our bodies at the same time. Humans are slow and each of them reacts differently. Sometimes all of the different energies are overwhelming and I leave them. If I feel that they have come together as a group, I come back to join them.

The beauty of horse and human bonding is evident each time I engage in the activities my caretakers create. In one experience, a person wants to move forward in her life; however she is being held back by boundaries she creates herself. By placing invisible walls around herself, she is stopping any forward growth. She stays in a safe refuge, refusing to engage with people and the opportunities present in her work and everyday life. She considers herself safe behind these barricades that block any and all emotion.

In the round pen, she immediately walks to the center and drops the whip so it is lying on the ground. Moving briskly she walks to the edge of the inside of the round pen where I am standing observing her actions. I am not uncomfortable being around the whip. In this work, people are taught that a whip is never used to hit a horse, but is provided as a tool to set boundaries for themselves if they feel uncomfortable when a horse approaches them.

In order to "talk" to her, I go to the center of the pen and put my muzzle in the tickly sand. Using my sensitive lips I pick up the whip, and balance it gently, bringing it back to her. Slowly inclining my head toward her, I show her that she is the one creating her own boundaries. I can see by her flushed face and changed posture, she "gets it." Holding herself back doesn't allow her heart space to be open to herself, others, and life. Now she can be her authentic self and live joyously in the moment.

Aria, another herdmate, wants me to share the experience she had with a young girl. The girl singled out Aria, as she is a very beautiful small horse. Thinking that she wouldn't be afraid due to the horse's dainty size, she confidently started to approach Aria. However, the young girl suddenly became afraid and started to breathe in short gasps from the top part of her chest; she froze in place and her eyes were round with fear. Aria focused on her own breathing and the young girl slowly matched her breathing to Aria's. A sense of peace came over the girl, providing an opportunity for her to connect with her inner being – a place she now knows and trusts.

Aria taught me about humans breathing. Breathing is the most important physical process for people on their path to enlightenment, a critical communication between the body and the universe. By learning the importance of breathing, even when sobbing, a person will release everything required for healing. You can let go of the mind when you are focused on the breath, opening your self to channel the energy of spirit. By allowing breath to flow throughout your body, you provide flexibility, an opening for universal knowing. A person can access a place of knowing by breathing slowly and deeply from their belly.

I, as a horse, know how to breathe correctly. Many humans who come to work with our herd have lost this ability, oftentimes forgetting the importance of their breath as their source of energy. Deep, slow breaths nourish and awaken all the cells in a human's body. These cells contain the human species' wisdom. By focusing on their breath and redirecting their mind from unnecessary mental chatter, they can achieve spiritual union with themselves and all of creation. They can then open their heart and learn to live from this place of love for themselves and others.

By using the wisdom of my horse ancestors, I can transition people and carry them to a higher stage of enlightenment. Previously humans looked at me and saw only physical freedom and power; now they are learning to sense the resonant energy field they can interact with.

One woman is so sad because she has lost someone of significance in her life. Feeling alone and abandoned, her body droops and her head hangs dejectedly. Approaching little by little, I stand in front of her, shielding her from the participants outside the round pen. Time stands still and a deep silence fills the arena. Slowly my presence starts to impact the space around her. She gradually lifts her head and looks at me with large blue eyes full of sorrow. I feel my heart expand in response.

Wanting her to know that she is not alone, I lightly rest my massive head on her delicate shoulder. At first her shoulder droops from the weight, then I feel her body start to respond to mine as she accepts our connection. She gazes into my large brown eye and sees her soul mirrored there in the deep, limpid pool. I move my muzzle and place it lightly on her chest, feeling her heart open. As the trust deepens, her tears start to fall from her young cheeks; tender tears of healing for her and for me.

While she is crying, I share her release by allowing hurts from long past to roll directly into Mother Earth. As her heart completely opens and connects to mine, there is tremendous healing energy flowing between us. I sigh, lick, and chew. I move my black head down her body to her legs and touch the rich earth with my lips. Lifting my huge foot gently into the air and putting it solidly on the ground, I encourage her to do the same so that she can be present in her body as it supports her on her path.

We start walking step by step together. At first she is hesitant, but the bearing of her body changes as she gains confidence. Head up, shoulders back, her eyes are alive and filled with hope. Walking at her side, shoulder-to-shoulder, we move together in authenticity and she finds that deep soul connection within herself. As we come to a close, her face is radiant as she thanks me. I can sense she has discovered she is never alone as long as she knows that connection.

One of my favorite activities is called active round pen. The first time, when I was led into the round pen and my caretaker started to lunge me, I was angry. I didn't want to run in senseless circles round and round. In my old life this was work to me. I was being told what to do and pushed to move. I stomped my foot in rage. I dug my heels in and refused to move, glaring at her defiantly. She patiently explained it was a new teaching role for me. I am the teacher for the person in the middle of the round pen who will ask me to walk, trot, turn, and then walk, trot again. I only go around the pen once in each gait and direction. She explained that the person sees by my behavior when they need to change something in their thoughts, approach to communication, emotional energy, or body awareness. When I feel or see a change in the human's posture or energy, then I know they are making a conscious shift within themselves, and I become more willing to engage on equal terms.

During the first session, a man enters the round pen for this activity. The man is asked to embody the activity so that the process reflects how he lives his life. The man walks into the round pen very full of himself. Thinking this is easy, his posture displays his arrogance, with his chest puffed out and a cocky set to his head. I can immediately see how unconnected he is with his body and his heart. He is in his head – listening to messages that have been playing and repeating in a continuous loop for a long time. I hear him say, "This is easy. Nothing to it. Piece of cake."

As he struts to the center of the round pen, the muscles in my body tighten in response. When he starts to command me to take action without initiating any sort of connection between us, I kick up my heels, turn in the opposite direction, and race head long around the round pen. Stopping, I turn my head in and look at him. The rigid way he is holding the lunge whip and the confident glitter in his eyes tell me he still isn't getting it.

Being contrary, I rapidly run in the opposite direction away from his pushing energy. With my chest heaving, I finally stop and face him, staring intently at him for a long time, trying to make him think about his actions. I watch the workshop facilitator come in and ask him to reflect on my behavior and see how that mirrors the way he is living his life. I quietly stand listening as the man speaks about how things in his life got away from him and he doesn't feel he was in control. When he begins to authentically tell the truth, his energy starts to come down to the center of his body and his heart opens. As his mind becomes calmer, his body relaxes, and his breathing becomes deeper. Finally, he connects with his body and works from his gut.

The man realizes he needs to engage not only his logical, rational brain, but his heart as well. When he asks from *this* place of connection, I quickly respond to his fluid movements and do as requested. He feels how quickly he goes into his head when he is challenged, and the difference it makes when he is centered. Now I feel he can lead his life.

We horses are incredible teachers. We teach by example. The way we live our lives is a valuable lesson we want to share. We live in the moment and invite humans to share this natural connection, where we all can fully participate in the joys and sorrows of life. Our hearts are open, creating a spiritual bond with ourselves and all those who have gone before us.

As humans learn to live authentically, they gain a deeper access to their inner body knowing, receiving immediate access to a greater wisdom through a wondrous connection with the universe.

We horses stand ready to share our insight, sparking humankind's ability to access their "higher self," their guide to a life of mindfulness and fulfillment. As we all connect to this energy, we join in the infinity loop of creation, leaping together as we journey to a realm of new possibilities and experiences.

I am Thor, and I share with you the wisdom of my horse ancestors.

Thor

Heartfelt thanks and gratitude goes to my life and business partner Andre, who has provided unstinting support on my journey, and of course, thanks to our amazing horses, both past and present. ~ Wendy

About
Wendy Golding

Wendy weaves together her love of horses, spiritual healing and leadership while creating a sacred place where healing and learning takes place on all levels for horses and people alike. Horses respond to the special energy found at her farm and fulfill their potential as teachers. They are treated as equal partners in a beautiful dance of healing where people find a deeper connection to their hearts and authentic selves.

Being passionate about horses all her life, Wendy took up riding again in her thirties and joined the Governor General's Horse Guards in Toronto, where she participated in the precision riding of military parades and the grace of musical rides. She loved the thrill of galloping down a field, sword at the ready, piercing a target and raising it high in triumph! Wendy went on to play the noble sport of polo, experiencing that incredible trust that exists between horse and rider, in mutual partnership.

After a bad fall and serious injury to her neck, Wendy sought another way to express her passion for life and stay connected to horses. Shamanism was part of the answer. Wendy learned the interconnectedness of all things and a way of seeing from the heart for the purpose of accessing spiritual guidance. After studying with inspirational teachers for nine years, Wendy is a Shamanic Coach, guiding others in fostering a deeper connection and relationship with nature and self.

Combining this healing modality with the wisdom of the horse opened a new world. Wendy was thrilled to discover the Epona Approach and Linda Kohanov. After experiencing first hand the powerful teachings from Linda and Kathleen Ingram, she knew that this was the magic she wanted to provide the world. Becoming an Epona Instructor she initiated a life long journey of service and joy.

As a vibrant, successful entrepreneur and co-owner of a multi-million dollar corporation, Wendy has worked in the corporate world for 25 years with Fortune 500 companies. Her natural leadership abilities led her to be President of the Jaycees - spearheading North American inaugural projects for the Chamber of Commerce, guest lecturer at Brock University, and a Director of the Governor General Horse Guards. These experiences paved the way for her consensual leadership dance within her three worlds.

Wendy melds her three passions (Horses, Shamanism, and Leadership) together in a beautiful matrix, walking her talk. She teaches that our lives and how we live them are interconnected,

Wendy and her life and business partner, Andre, founded Horse Spirit Connections located near Toronto, Canada. This not-for-profit corporation supports Facilitated Equine Experiential Learning (FEEL) services and programs including transformational personal development workshops for people of all ages, and the Spirit of Leadership program for organizations and corporations. Wendy invites you to awaken your spirit at www.HorseSpiritConnections.com.

Author Contact Information

Lisa Dee	www.vistacaballo.com
Wendy Golding	www.horsespiritconnections.com
Karen Head	www.equinection.org
Holli Lyons	www.lyonsgait.com
Stormy May	www.stormymay.com
Mary Beth Meyers	www.harmonicriding.com
Melisa Pearce	www.touchedbyahorse.com
Kathy Pike	www.coachingwithhorses.com
Anna Twinney	www.reachouttohorses.com
Susan Williams	www.windhorseone.com